# Last Impressions:
# Unforgettable Closings
# for Youth Meetings

**Group**
Loveland, Colorado

■■■■■■■■■■■■■■■■■■■■■■■■■■■■■■■■■■■■■

**Last Impressions: Unforgettable Closings for Youth Meetings**
Copyright © 1996 Group Publishing, Inc.

**Credits**
Editor: Pamela J. Shoup
Creative Products Director: Joani Schultz
Copy Editor: Amy Simpson
Editorial Assistant: Kerri Nance
Art Director: Lisa Chandler
Cover Art Director: Liz Howe
Designer: Lisa Chandler
Computer Graphic Artist: Kari K. Monson
Cover Photographers: Telegraph Colour Library/FPG International and Craig DeMartino
Cover Photo Illustrator: Randy Miller
Illustrator: Kari K. Monson
Production Manager: Ann Marie Gordon

Unless otherwise noted, Scriptures quoted from The Youth Bible, New Century Version, copyright © 1991 by Word Publishing, Dallas, Texas 75039. Used by permission.

**Library of Congress Cataloging-in-Publication Data**
Last Impressions : unforgettable closings for youth meetings.
      p.        cm.
   ISBN 1-55945-6299
   1. Church group work with youth.
BV4447.L37 1996
268'.433--dc20                                   95-49541
                                                             CIP

10 9 8 7 6 5 4 3 2 1       05 04 03 02 01 00 99 98 97 96

Printed in the United States of America.

# Table of Contents

## Affirming Closings 10

## Youth-Issue Closings 25

## High-Energy Closings 50

# Prayerful Closings 68

## Servanthood Closings 88

## Thoughtful Closings 95

# Introduction

*D*o *your youth meetings fizzle out at the end? As your meetings wind down, do teenagers drift away before you're ready for them to leave? Do you feel as if your teenagers are leaving with a good grasp on the day's lesson? Have you made a lasting impression on them?*

*We all want to send our kids home with a little more knowledge than they came in with—plus challenges for them to meet, affirmations to make them feel special, stronger faith, a sense of community, and, of course, smiles on their faces. Having a specific closing for each meeting is like wrapping up the meeting in a package. It signals kids that the meeting is over, it often reinforces the point taught in the lesson, and it may become a ritual for your group as your teenagers look forward to the creative closings you come up with each week.*

*If you have problems with fizzle-and-drift endings, here is help! Call it the grand finale, the big finish, the last hurrah for any youth meeting.* **Last Impressions: Unforgettable Closings for Youth Meetings** *features over 170 ideas for meetings with any kind of theme. The activities require very little preparation time and few or no supplies.*

*In* **Last Impressions: Unforgettable Closings for Youth Meetings,** *you'll find youth-issue closings about true love, friendship, and cliques. The chapter on high-energy closings includes ideas for parties, games, and themes including peer pressure and dating. In the chapters on affirming and prayerful closings, you'll find just that—loads of affirmations and lots of ideas for closing your meetings with prayer. The section on thoughtful closings deals with topics including accepting God's grace, eternal life, and knowing Jesus. If you want your kids to become better servants, try a servanthood closing.*

*Each activity has a list of the supplies you'll need and an appropriate Scripture reference that either is used in the closing or relates to the closing topic. In the back of this book, you'll find a Scripture index to help you tie in closings to most meeting topics.*

■■■■■■■■■■■■■■■■■■■■■■■■■■■■■■■■■■■■■■■■■

*The ideas in this book are proven successful closings, submitted by youth leaders and previously published in GROUP Magazine and in various books and curriculum published by Group Publishing.* **Last Impressions: Unforgettable Closings for Youth Meetings** *is a compilation of closing activities from more than 100 youth leaders and Group authors and editors. Although we can't list all the contributors to this book, we do thank them for their ideas and their dedication to sharing their faith, their knowledge, and their time with teenagers.*

*Read on, and you're sure to find loads of ideas to leave lasting impressions with your teenagers.*

■■■■■■■■■■■■■■■■■■■■■■■■■■■■■■■■■■

# Affirming Closings

"There are different kinds of gifts, but they are all
from the same Spirit"
(1 CORINTHIANS 12:4).

*Teenagers really need occasional affirmations to boost their self-esteem. A never-fail closing to your youth group meeting is one that makes everyone feel good and feel accepted. And to grow in their faith, kids need to know that God has given each of them special gifts and is always there for them.*

## ■ Your Future ■

**PURPOSE:** *to understand that they can do anything through God's power*

**SCRIPTURE:** *Philippians 4:13*

**SUPPLIES:** *none*

Form groups of three or four. Say: **Tell each person in your group one great thing that you think he or she has the potential to do in the future. For example, you might say, "You have the potential to be a great leader."**

After the conversation dies down, close with prayer, asking God to help kids believe that God's power can do great things through them.

## ■ Bright Spots ■

**PURPOSE:** *to know that God has hope and plans for them*

**SCRIPTURE:** *Jeremiah 29:11*

**SUPPLIES:** *Bibles, 5-inch circles of brightly colored construction paper, and markers*

In groups of three or four, read aloud Jeremiah 29:11. Then have each teenager write about one "bright spot" from his or her week on a 5-inch circle of construction paper and share it in the small group. After everyone has shared, give each person a second bright spot and have kids write, "I have tons of hope for you, and so does God." Encourage each student to take the bright spot and give it to another person who needs encouragement during the week.

Close with a prayer or a song, thanking God for caring about us.

## • It's a Wonderful Life! •

**PURPOSE:** *to discover what makes them unique and important*

**SCRIPTURE:** *1 Corinthians 12:1-11*

**SUPPLIES:** *pencils, photocopies of the "It's a Wonderful Life!" card, and an ink pad*

Give each person a pencil and a photocopy of the "It's a Wonderful Life!" card. After the teenagers have completed the cards, have each person "sign" his or her card with a fingerprint, showing uniqueness and individuality. Have kids get with partners and read their cards. Encourage kids to carry their cards with them.

Close in prayer, thanking God for each person's life and asking that kids will have strength to "choose life."

# It's a Wonderful Life

### (and I'm special!)

I am unique and important because _____.

I have the special gift/talent of _____.

A thing I love to do is _____.

I have a special relationship with _____.

A dream I have is _____.

One thing I like about me is _____.

■ ■ ■ ■ ■ ■ ■ ■ ■ ■ ■ ■ ■ ■ ■ ■ ■ ■ ■ ■ ■ ■ ■ ■ ■ ■ ■ ■ ■ ■ ■ ■ ■ ■ ■ ■ ■ ■ ■

# ▪ A New Respect ▪

**PURPOSE:** *to show respect for one another*

**SCRIPTURE:** *Romans 14:10*

**SUPPLIES:** *a beach ball*

Have kids form a circle, and place a beach ball in the middle of the circle.

Say: **Learning to respect others isn't always easy. Although we may not respect the actions of others, we can still follow God's Word and respect them by not judging them.**

Pick up the beach ball and toss it to someone. Have kids continue tossing the ball around the circle. As kids toss the ball to one another, have them complete this sentence: "I respect you because . . . " After a couple of minutes, place the ball in the center of the circle again and close with prayer.

# ▪ What's Inside ▪

**PURPOSE:** *to look within themselves to discover the gifts God has given them*

**SCRIPTURE:** *Psalm 139:13-16*

**SUPPLIES:** *a Bible, newsprint, markers, tape, and index cards*

List the following words on a sheet of newsprint: understanding, gentle, cheerful, peacemaking, dependable, loving, thoughtful, helpful, persistent, faithful, tenderhearted, encouraging, patient, forgiving, kind, joyful, honest, and loyal. Label the sheet of newsprint "What's Inside?"

Tape the "What's Inside?" list to a wall. Give each person an index card and a marker. Have kids write on each card two words from the "What's Inside?" list that describe what they're like inside. Have them tape their cards to the front of their shirts and form a circle.

Ask a volunteer to read aloud Psalm 139:13-16. Then, starting with the person on your right, have each student affirm the person on the right, using the two words he or she chose. Kids should say, "Thanks, God, that (name) is _____ and _____." Have kids continue around the circle until everyone has been affirmed. Close by asking God to help your kids discover their unique abilities.

## ▪ Anonymous Prophecies ▪

**PURPOSE:** *to predict great things for fellow class members, based on their talents*

**SCRIPTURE:** *Philippians 4:13*

**SUPPLIES:** *pencils, index cards, and a basket*

Have the group form a circle, and give each person a pencil and an index card. Have kids write their names on the cards, then put all the cards in a basket. Pass the basket around the circle and have everyone draw a name.

Say: **Use the other side of the card to write a "prophecy" about the person whose name you've drawn. Write about the way you think his or her gifts will develop and how God will use this person in the future. Be sure to make this prophecy a positive one.** For example, kids might write, "You'll be a great leader in the church someday" or "You'll be a respected artist someday."

When all the prophecies have been written, collect the cards again, then return each card to the person whose name is on the card. Give kids a few moments to read the anonymous prophecies their friends have written. Then gather for prayer. Have each student thank God for the person on his or her left.

## ▪ Support Net ▪

**PURPOSE:** *to support one another in their faith in the face of ridicule*

**SCRIPTURE:** *2 Corinthians 4:16-18*

**SUPPLIES:** *index cards, pencils, and tape*

Have kids form a circle. Place pencils and a handful of index cards on the floor in the center of the circle. Say: **We all have aspects of our faith—such as patience, love for others, and trust in God—that can help us deal with ridicule. Think about the person on your left and what his or her strengths are. Then pick up a card and a pencil and write on the card one strength you see in the person on your left. Give the card to that person. Then write a card for at least one other person in the circle.**

When each person has at least one card, tell teenagers to place the cards next to each other on the floor in the center of the circle. Then have kids help you tape the cards together to form a "net." Have kids huddle together and hold the net in the center of the circle.

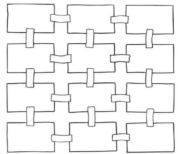

Say: **By supporting each other with encouragement and positive words, we form a net that can help us feel confident in our faith when others challenge it.**

Have volunteers close in prayer, asking God to help them use their strengths as a net to help when they face persecution and to help them respond in loving ways to people who ridicule them.

# • Free Hugs •

**PURPOSE:** *to show love to your youth group members*

**SCRIPTURE:** *John 15:12*

**SUPPLIES:** *none*

At the end of your youth group meeting, announce that free hugs will be given as people leave. Have both a female and a male youth worker at the exit door, and have the female hug the girls and the male hug the guys. This is a great way to express love to kids who might not receive any—and it can make their day or week.

# • Giving Thanks •

**PURPOSE:** *to express thanks to friends*

**SCRIPTURE:** *1 Thessalonians 5:18*

**SUPPLIES:** *thank you cards and pencils*

Give each person a thank you card and a pencil. Have kids form pairs, and have partners write thank you notes to each other; for example, they may write something like "Thanks for being available when I need to talk to someone." Have partners exchange and keep the cards.

As a closing prayer, form a circle and have kids call out things they're thankful for.

# · Affirming Whispers ·

**PURPOSE:** *to resist the temptation to gossip*

**SCRIPTURE:** *Psalm 55:20-22*

**SUPPLIES:** *a Bible*

Have kids form a circle, then whisper something affirming to the person on your left. Tell him or her to do the same for the next person. When the whispered words of appreciation come back around to you, read Psalm 55:20-22 aloud. Close the meeting in prayer, asking God to give group members strength to resist the temptation to gossip.

# · "Body Beautiful" Awards ·

**PURPOSE:** *to affirm one another as parts of the body of Christ*

**SCRIPTURE:** *Romans 12:4-8 and 1 Corinthians 12:12-27*

**SUPPLIES:** *construction paper, glue, markers, and several photocopies of the " 'Body Beautiful' Awards" handout (p. 16)*

Have kids arrange themselves in a circle, sitting in order according to their birthdays. Set out the award pictures from the photocopies of the " 'Body Beautiful' Awards" handout (p. 16) in the middle of the circle, and give each person a sheet of construction paper, glue, and a marker. Have each teenager create a "Body Beautiful" award for the person on his or her right. Have kids choose pictures, glue them to their construction paper, then write why they chose those pictures for the people on their right. For example, someone may write, "Mandy, I give you this 'Body Beautiful' hand award because you're always willing to lend a helping hand to anyone who asks. Love, Beth."

After all the kids have received their awards, congratulate them on working together to become Christ's beautiful body—the church. Encourage kids to keep their awards as reminders of their vital roles in Christ's body.

Close with prayer, asking God to give kids strength to fulfill their commitments and to become even more active parts of Christ's body in the world.

# "Body Beautiful" Awards

*Cut along the dotted lines to separate the pictures.*

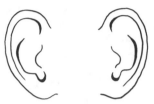

"Ear"resistible

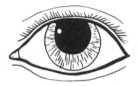

"Eye" admire you

"Hand"y to have around

Unde"feet"able

# • Gift of Life •

**PURPOSE:** *to express the simple joys in life*

**SCRIPTURE:** *Psalm 92:1-4*

**SUPPLIES:** *balloons, a cassette player or CD player, and a cassette tape or CD of music by a popular Christian artist*

Play a cassette tape or CD of music by a popular Christian artist and have each person blow up and tie off a balloon. Have kids bat the balloons around the room while the music plays.

After a few minutes, say: **God gave each one of us a wonderful life to live. Just as the simple joy of playing with balloons can help us feel good about ourselves, learning to love God more can help us love life more too.**

Have kids form pairs, and have each pair grab two balloons. Tell each teenager to say one thing he or she appreciates about his or her partner then pop a balloon as an exclamation mark for that appreciation. Close the meeting by having kids offer one-word prayers of thanks to God for the gift of life.

# • I Believe in You •

**PURPOSE:** *to encourage each other to achieve their dreams with God's help*

**SCRIPTURE:** *1 John 5:14-15*

**SUPPLIES:** *a Bible*

Have kids form pairs, and have partners describe dreams they have and their goals to reach those dreams. Then have each person tell one thing about the partner's personality that will help that person achieve his or her dream, such as "You always see the humor in what happens. You'll be able to handle the hard work needed to achieve your dream."

When everyone has shared, have pairs close with prayer, asking God to help them achieve their dreams.

Close by reading aloud 1 John 5:14-15, assuring kids that God hears and answers their prayers.

■ ■ ■ ■ ■ ■ ■ ■ ■ ■ ■ ■ ■ ■ ■ ■ ■ ■ ■ ■ ■ ■ ■ ■ ■ ■ ■ ■ ■ ■ ■ ■ ■ ■ ■ ■

# ▪ Faith From A to Z ▪

**PURPOSE:** *to affirm one another for their faith*

**SCRIPTURE:** *Matthew 21:21*

**SUPPLIES:** *none*

Have kids form a circle and play an encouragement game. Have each person say to the person on his or her right: "You have a(n) _____ faith." Let kids fill in the blank with an adjective starting with A (amazing, astonishing, absolutely wonderful). Have a few kids continue, then have people start filling in the blank with adjectives beginning with B (beautiful, basically dynamic). Change letters from time to time if kids run out of adjectives.

Close by saying: **God will help us share our faith with our friends. Let's trust him to guide us.**

# ▪ United We Stand ▪

**PURPOSE:** *to recognize one another for overcoming evil in the world*

**SCRIPTURE:** *Jeremiah 18:8*

**SUPPLIES:** *none*

Have kids gather in a huddle. Tell them to form pairs by reaching in with their right hands and each grabbing someone else's hand. One at a time, have each person tell one way his or her partner helps overcome evil in the world by doing good.

Close with prayer, thanking God for the power to overcome evil in the world. One pair at a time, have partners say "amen" as they unclasp their hands.

# ▪ Friendship Commitment ▪

**PURPOSE:** *to strengthen qualities of friendship in themselves*

**SCRIPTURE:** *Ruth 1:16*

**SUPPLIES:** *uninflated balloons, slips of paper, and pencils*

Distribute an uninflated balloon, a slip of paper, and a pencil to each person.

Say: **Let's close this meeting by talking about the qualities of a good friend. What are some qualities you like your friends to**

**have?** Allow kids to mention various traits such as loyalty, honesty, kindness, or love. Say: **On your slip of paper write one quality of friendship you want to develop or strengthen in yourself.**

Have each person place his or her slip of paper inside a balloon then inflate the balloon and tie it off. Tell kids to take the balloons home.

Say: **When your balloon loses its air, cut it open and read the paper as a reminder of your desire to improve a friendship-building quality.**

Close by having each teenager say something positive to at least one other person about that person's ability to be a friend. Then pray together, thanking God for good friendships.

## ▪ Best Friends ▪

**PURPOSE:** *to learn why God is their friend*

**SCRIPTURE:** *John 15:15-16*

**SUPPLIES:** *a Bible*

Form two groups and have each group form a tight circle. One group will represent "God" and the other themselves. The "God" group will go first and complete this statement: "I appreciate you, (name of person in other group), because you are (kind to visitors, friendly, etc.)." Then the other group will complete the statement for the "God" group, saying something such as "I appreciate you, God, because you care for me." Let kids share back and forth as long as they have ideas. Then have them switch roles and share back and forth again. Ask:

● **How did you feel during this experience?**

● **In what ways was this experience like the friendship each one of you could have with God?**

Read aloud John 15:15 16. Ask:

● **According to this passage, why does Jesus call us friends?**

Have kids form pairs, and have each partner commit to be a friend and show God's love in some way to another person this week. Have pairs close in prayer. Say: **God chose you to be his friends. Because of his love, we follow his command to love each other.**

# ▪ The Dove ▪

**PURPOSE:** *to recognize their spiritual gifts*

**SCRIPTURE:** *1 Corinthians 12:4-7*

**SUPPLIES:** *a Bible, photocopies of the "Dove" handout (p. 21), scissors, and pencils*

Have kids form pairs. Give each person a photocopy of the "Dove" handout (p. 21) and a pencil. Have each teenager cut out a dove and write his or her partner's name on it. Say: **The dove is a symbol of the Holy Spirit. On the back of your dove, list gifts and abilities you see in your partner. You may want to include something positive about the person that makes him or her a good friend.**

Read aloud 1 Corinthians 12:4-7 and have kids present the doves to their partners. Encourage teenagers to use the doves as bookmarks in their Bibles to remind them of the spiritual gifts they've been given.

# ▪ Cover of the Rolled Stone ▪

**PURPOSE:** *to celebrate their unique qualities by posting their portraits on a magazine cover*

**SCRIPTURE:** *Mark 16:3-4*

**SUPPLIES:** *newsprint, markers, and paper*

Say: **Musicians and other public figures often think they've "made it" when they get their pictures on the cover of Rolling Stone magazine. But this kind of popularity is fleeting. Just as Jesus was at one time popular and later unpopular, so our popularity comes and goes. But Jesus' resurrection proves that God thinks we're each important. Jesus' "rolled stone" away from the grave is our proof.**

Have kids use newsprint and markers to design a wall-sized "Rolled Stone" magazine cover. Then have each person draw a self-portrait on a sheet of paper. In a closing ceremony, have each teenager walk up to the magazine cover and tape his or her self-portrait to the newsprint. Close with a prayer, thanking God that he sees each person as important and special.

# Dove

■ ■ ■ ■ ■ ■ ■ ■ ■ ■ ■ ■ ■ ■ ■ ■ ■ ■ ■ ■ ■ ■ ■ ■ ■ ■ ■ ■ ■ ■ ■ ■ ■ ■ ■ ■ ■

# ▪ Friendly Opportunities ▪

**PURPOSE:** *to share their faith with others*

**SCRIPTURE:** *Proverbs 17:17; Proverbs 18:24; and John 15:13,15*

**SUPPLIES:** *Bibles*

Say: **Youth group is a special place. It's where you develop new friendships, build positive relationships, search out the meaning of your faith, and grow closer to Christ.**

**It's also where friendship evangelism begins—where you can share your faith with a friend you bring and where you can reach out to someone with Jesus' love. By reaching out to others, you'll develop friendships that model the biblical understanding of God's love.**

Have kids form trios then read and discuss these Scriptures about friendship: Proverbs 18:24; Proverbs 17:17; and John 15:13, 15. Ask:

● **What kinds of qualities will true friends show?**
● **Would you really die for friends? When and why?**
● **What's the best thing you can do for your friends?**

Say: **The conclusion is simple: Friends bring friends to Christ. Friendship is an opportunity to share with others your living, personal faith in Jesus Christ.**

Have kids state ways they might share their faith this coming week. Close with a group hug.

# ▪ Lookin' Good (For Girls Only) ▪

**PURPOSE:** *to boost self-esteem for the girls in your group*

**SCRIPTURE:** *Proverbs 31:30-31*

**SUPPLIES:** *index cards, pencils, and tape*

Have girls form pairs, and give each girl five index cards, a pencil, and tape. Have each person write one positive thing about her partner on each card. Then have girls tape the cards to the appropriate areas of their partners' bodies and tell what they've written and why. For example, someone might tape a card to a girl's head because she's a good thinker or to her feet because she always hurries to help people.

After every girl has cards taped to her, have girls model their

■ ■ ■ ■ ■ ■ ■ ■ ■ ■ ■ ■ ■ ■ ■ ■ ■ ■ ■ ■ ■ ■ ■ ■ ■ ■ ■ ■ ■ ■ ■

cards. As girls model, have the other girls cheer for them. Then close with a prayer, thanking God for cheering us on when our self-esteem is low.

## ■ Making the Grade ■

**PURPOSE:** *to point out God's gifts in one another*

**SCRIPTURE:** *Psalm 23 and Romans 12:3-8*

**SUPPLIES:** *a Bible, paper, pencils, a cassette player or CD player, and a cassette tape or CD of soft music*

Have each person write his or her name at the top of a piece of paper then write these grades in large letters below the name: A, B, C, D, and F. Have kids form groups of four or five and pass their papers around their groups. When each person receives someone's paper, he or she must write five affirming and encouraging words to that person, each starting with a different grade letter. For example, someone might write, "Artistic, Bubbly, Caring, Dependable, Fun."

Have team members form a circle on the floor by lying on their backs with their heads together in the middle. Take time to relax and be quiet. Play soft background music. Then read aloud Psalm 23 followed by Romans 12:3-8 as a closing prayer.

## ■ My Superhero Abilities ■

**PURPOSE:** *to recognize their abilities to help others*

**SCRIPTURE:** *Romans 12:6-8*

**SUPPLIES:** *paper, markers, scissors, and hero sandwiches*

Give each teenager a sheet of paper, a marker, and scissors to use to create a superhero emblem.

After kids have created their emblems, have them form pairs. Have partners discuss the abilities they have to help others in need. Have each student write two or three of these abilities on his or her emblem. Then have partners take turns praying for each other, asking God to strengthen their gifts for doing God's will. Serve hero sandwiches after the meeting.

# ■ Something Special in a Name ■

**PURPOSE:** *to affirm one another with an acrostic exercise*

**SCRIPTURE:** *Luke 10:20*

**SUPPLIES:** *pencils and paper*

Have kids form a circle, and distribute pencils and sheets of paper.

Say: **One thing that's unique about you is your name. Turn your paper horizontally and write your name across it in big letters. We're going to build acrostics around your name to show how you are uniquely and wonderfully made.**

When kids have written their names, have them put their papers on the floor and rotate one position to the left. Kids will add one word or phrase describing a positive quality of the person whose name appears on the paper in front of them. Have kids keep going in this rotation until everyone's acrostic is complete. Shorter names will be finished first. Kids with really long names may choose to use nicknames.

Here is a sample acrostic:

```
g                     h
R  I  C  K    T  H  O  M  P  S  O  N
e  n  l  i    r  a  n  u  a  u  u  i
a  t  e  n    a  p  e  s  t  p  t  c
t  e  v  d    c  p  s  i  i  e  g  e
   r  e        k  y  t  c  e  r  o
   e  r            t  c  e  r  o
   s           s      i  n     i  g
   t           t      a  t     n  u
   i           a      n        g  y
   n           r
   g
```

Have kids return to their own papers. Ask:

● **How does it feel to read the positive qualities that other kids see in you?**

Say: **Keep your paper for future reference. When you get down on yourself, you can use this as a reminder of what a wonderful person you are!**

■ ■ ■ ■ ■ ■ ■ ■ ■ ■ ■ ■ ■ ■ ■ ■ ■ ■ ■ ■ ■ ■ ■ ■ ■ ■ ■ ■ ■ ■ ■ ■

# Youth-Issue Closings

"I will be with you always, even until the end of this age"
(MATTHEW 28:20B).

*T*eenagers worry about many issues—school, friends, families, dating, and love, to name a few. By closing your meetings with issues of special interest to your teenagers and promoting awareness of the world they live in, you will strengthen your relationship with your kids, the relationships among your group members, and teenagers' relationships with God.

## ■ Personal Rebellion ■

**PURPOSE:** *to turn negative rebellion into something positive*

**SCRIPTURE:** *Jonah 1:1-3*

**SUPPLIES:** *index cards and pencils*

As you distribute index cards and pencils, say: **Write about one negative way you've rebelled against your parents, your teachers, or others this past week. Don't write your name on the card.**

Collect the cards, mix them up, and redistribute them. Be sure everyone has someone else's card. Ask teenagers to read aloud the rebellion cards they were given. As a group, have kids discuss ways to turn each negative form of rebellion into something positive. Tell kids to pray silently for the people who wrote the rebellion cards they were given. Close with a prayer, asking God to turn negative rebellion into positive rebellion.

## ■ True-Love Truths ■

**PURPOSE:** *to understand what true love really is*

**SCRIPTURE:** *1 Corinthians 13:4-7 and 1 John 4:7-12*

**SUPPLIES:** *Bibles, paper, pencils, and photocopies of the "Love Is More Than a Feeling" handout (p. 27)*

Have kids form groups of no more than four. Give each group a sheet of paper, a pencil, and a Bible. Say: **Read 1 John 4:7-12 and 1 Corinthians 13:4-7, then write on your paper a true-love truth; for example, you could write, "True love is God's love for us."**

Have volunteers read their groups' true-love truths. Then say: **True love is God's love. Find someone who loves you and who you love with the true love described in 1 Corinthians 13:4-7 and 1 John 4:7-12. Don't settle for anything less.**

Distribute photocopies of the "Love Is More Than a Feeling" handout (p. 27) and have teenagers read the script aloud to close the meeting.

## ▪ Forever Friends ▪

**PURPOSE:** *to explore qualities of lasting friendship*

**SCRIPTURE:** *John 3:16 and John 15:13*

**SUPPLIES:** *a Bible*

Have kids form pairs. Have partners say at least one thing that they believe makes friendships last, such as honesty, patience, and love. Then have kids pray that their partners exhibit those qualities in their own friendships.

Close by reading John 3:16 and John 15:13 to remind kids about Jesus' ultimate act of friendship.

## ▪ Shepherd Me, Lord ▪

**PURPOSE:** *to take comfort in God's presence during mood swings*

**SCRIPTURE:** *Psalm 23*

**SUPPLIES:** *a Bible, photocopies of the "Blues-Buster Tips" handout (p. 28), paper, and markers*

Say: **Although we have high mood swings and low mood swings—such as depression—are often the most difficult to deal with. One way to deal with our mood swings is to remember that God is always with us, even in the lowest valleys.**

Give each person a sheet of paper, a marker, and a photocopy of the "Blues-Buster Tips" handout (p. 28), and have kids draw a line down the middle of their papers.

*(continued on p. 28)*

# Love Is More Than a Feeling

**Girls:** Love is more than a feeling.

**Guys:** Love is a decision.

**Girls:** A decision based on . . .

**Guys:** more than an attraction to a person,

**Girls:** love is a careful process

**Guys:** of reasoning and commitment.

**Girls:** You think it through.

**Guys:** You weigh all the facts.

**Girls:** You make a conscious choice.

**Guys:** Marriages based on feelings alone

**Girls:** stand on dangerous ground.

**Guys:** That's because feelings can and will change.

**Girls:** But a love based on a decision and on commitment

**Guys:** will withstand the changing winds of feelings.

**Girls:** God shows us how to love each other;

**Guys:** God sticks by us no matter what,

**Girls:** through all sorts of feelings.

**Guys:** That's God's unconditional love.

**Girls:** Love is more than a feeling.

**Guys:** Love is a decision.

On the left side of their papers, have kids draw pictures representing situations in which they have low mood swings. On the right side of their papers, have each person draw a picture of himself or herself doing one of the "Blues-Buster Tips" to level out that mood swing.

Afterward, read aloud Psalm 23. Ask:

● **How does knowing that God is with you help you deal with your mood swings?**

● **What are some "green pastures" and "calm waters" in your life that help to restore your soul?**

Say: **Write the reference "Psalm 23" on the left side of your picture. Take your picture home. When you feel down, use it to remind you that God is still your shepherd.**

Close in prayer.

# Blues-Buster Tips

● Exercise—walk, run, or play basketball.

● Be good to yourself. Get some rest and eat a good meal.

● Celebrate small victories. Treat yourself to a banana split when you ace that math test or finish a project.

● Help someone in need.

● Write a thank you note to someone who helps you.

● Talk to a trusted adult friend outside your family.

● Watch how you react to others. Don't let them control your feelings.

● List your fears and worries. Pray about them each day.

● List the good things in your life and thank God for them.

# ■ A Prayer to Share ■

**PURPOSE:** *to write a letter to God, asking for better communication with their parents*

**SCRIPTURE:** *Exodus 20:12*

**SUPPLIES:** *paper and pencils*

Say: **If you truly want better communication with your parents, you must take the first step and ask for it.**

Distribute sheets of paper and pencils. Have kids write short letters to God, explaining their desire to communicate better with their parents. Then have kids promise to deliver their letters to their parents, establishing a starting place for discussion about improved communication. Close in prayer, asking God to help improve communication in the kids' families.

# ■ A Promise of Peace ■

**PURPOSE:** *to ask for God's peace in dealing with stress*

**SCRIPTURE:** *John 16:33*

**SUPPLIES:** *a Bible*

Have kids form a circle. Ask each person to call out one or two words that describe stress, such as "homework" or "expectations." Read aloud John 16:33. Close in prayer, thanking God for his peace in the midst of stress.

# ■ Media Masters ■

**PURPOSE:** *to create a filter to use in choosing songs, movies, and TV shows*

**SCRIPTURE:** *Philippians 4:8*

**SUPPLIES:** *newsprint, markers, paper, and pencils*

Say: **To be a "media master," you have to know how to evaluate the appropriateness of songs, movies, and TV shows. Together let's create a "filter" to use in choosing media to listen to or to view.**

Have kids brainstorm ideas for some filters to use when choosing what to watch or listen to. For example, they may ask themselves, "If Jesus were sitting next to me, would I be watching that movie?"

■■■■■■■■■■■■■■■■■■■■■■■■■■■■■■■■■■■■■■■■■■

Have a volunteer write the filter ideas on newsprint. Then have kids sign the newsprint as a commitment to try out these filters during the coming week. Give kids sheets of paper and pencils so they can copy the filters for their own use.

Close in prayer, asking God to help kids become media masters and make good decisions about movies, music, and television.

## ■ Lean on Me ■

**PURPOSE:** *to experience the fact that none of us stands alone*

**SCRIPTURE:** *Luke 11:23*

**SUPPLIES:** *none*

Have kids form a circle and join hands. On "go," have everyone in the group slowly lean backward, relying on each other's grip to hold them up. Repeat the motion several times, then ask:

● **How does this circle symbolize our dependence on each other?**

Say: **As we've just experienced by leaning back in this circle, none of us can stand alone. We need each other to keep us from falling, and we need to stand together for God.**

Close with a prayer of thanks for each person in the room.

## ■ My Decision ■

**PURPOSE:** *to ask for God's guidance in making tough decisions*

**SCRIPTURE:** *Psalm 73:24 and James 4:7*

**SUPPLIES:** *paper, pencils, and a paper sack*

Give each person a sheet of paper and a pencil. Say: **Everyone has tough decisions to make. Think about a tough decision you're facing right now or you may have to face in the future. Write it on your paper and keep it to yourself.**

Place the sheets of paper in a paper sack. Have each person pull out a sheet of paper and commit to pray during the week for the person whose decision is described on the paper. Close by asking for God's guidance in making the tough decisions of life.

■ ■ ■ ■ ■ ■ ■ ■ ■ ■ ■ ■ ■ ■ ■ ■ ■ ■ ■ ■ ■ ■ ■ ■ ■ ■ ■ ■ ■ ■ ■ ■ ■

## ▪ Holy Spirit, Lead Us ▪

**PURPOSE:** *to ask for guidance from the Holy Spirit in turning away from bad habits*

**SCRIPTURE:** *Romans 8:14*

**SUPPLIES:** *a Bible*

Have kids form a circle for a prayer. Ask volunteers to mention some of the bad habits they or friends and family members have. Ask God to help you and your group members make the right choices and turn away from bad habits. Have a volunteer read aloud Romans 8:14 as a closing meditation, and discuss with the kids how God's Spirit leads them.

## ▪ Disciples Indeed ▪

**PURPOSE:** *to share their struggles as Jesus' disciples shared theirs*

**SCRIPTURE:** *Ecclesiastes 4:9-10*

**SUPPLIES:** *none*

Have kids form pairs. Say: **Jesus' disciples lived out their faith by supporting each other and struggling through the tough times together.**

Have kids take one or two minutes to tell their partners about the questions or problems they're struggling with. Then have partners pray for each other, asking for God's guidance in each of the specific areas mentioned.

Close by having kids stand in a circle and give each other a group hug to symbolize that they're all working together to become God's disciples.

## ▪ Involving God ▪

**PURPOSE:** *to ask for God's help in dealing with school issues*

**SCRIPTURE:** *Proverbs 2:1-6 and Matthew 7:7-8*

**SUPPLIES:** *a Bible, paper, and pencils*

Read aloud Matthew 7:7-8. Ask:

● **If you pray for good grades, will you get them? Why or why not?**

■ ■ ■ ■ ■ ■ ■ ■ ■ ■ ■ ■ ■ ■ ■ ■ ■ ■ ■ ■ ■ ■ ■ ■ ■ ■ ■ ■ ■ ■ ■ ■ ■ ■ ■

● If you pray for athletic, musical, or artistic ability, will you get it? Why or why not?

● What else could you pray for that might help you with your grades?

Distribute sheets of paper and pencils. Assign a letter of the alphabet to each person. As a prayer, have each person write then read a thought of help, encouragement, or hope for school, each one beginning with the letter that person has been given. For example, a person with the letter B could write, "Believe that God cares about you." A person with the letter K could say, "Know that you can do all things through Christ's strength." Conclude by reading Proverbs 2:1-6.

## ■ Gospel Scan ■

**PURPOSE:** *to learn how Jesus might have responded to people with AIDS*

**SCRIPTURE:** *Luke 6:37-42 and Luke 17:11-19*

**SUPPLIES:** *Bibles, matches, and a candle*

Give each person a Bible. Have kids scan the Gospels, pointing out stories of Jesus' life that teach us how to respond to AIDS victims and to fears about AIDS. For example, look at the passage in Luke 6:37-42 about judging others and the story of the 10 lepers in Luke 17:11-19. Use a New Century Version Bible or a similar one with subheads, which help highlight stories.

Pass a lighted candle around the group. When each person receives the candle, have him or her say a prayer concerning AIDS and pass the candle to the next person.

## ■ Hope for the Future ■

**PURPOSE:** *to discover the promise of hope in the next world*

**SCRIPTURE:** *Revelation 21:1-5*

**SUPPLIES:** *a Bible*

Say: **The world we live in is imperfect. And for reasons we can't fully understand, God allows both good and bad people to experience pleasure and pain. But God has also given Christians a great hope of a perfect world without pain and suffering.**

Have someone read aloud Revelation 21:1-5. Have kids tell what that passage means to them. Then have each person think of a message of hope, such as "Be comforted because the kingdom is coming and soon your pain will be gone." Have kids form a circle. Then have each person say his or her message of hope to the person directly across the circle.

To close, have kids complete the following "hope" prayer, filling in the blanks with information describing situations that they or their loved ones are experiencing: **Dear God, when I think of the bad things that happen in the world, such as** (have kids respond), **I feel** (have kids respond). **But I know you love us and promise a new world without pain. As I wait for that day with feelings of** (have kids respond), **give me patience in these difficult times.**

## ▪ Smoking Situations ▪

**PURPOSE:** *to encourage teenagers to reject smoking*

**SCRIPTURE:** *1 Corinthians 3:16*

**SUPPLIES:** *a wastebasket and cigarette ads from magazines*

Have kids form small groups, and give each group two or three cigarette ads from magazines. Have kids imagine themselves being offered a cigarette in the situation shown in each ad. Have groups think of an appropriate response for each of their ads; for example, "I know you're supposed to look glamorous when you smoke, but no thanks. I can look just as good without smoking." Let each group report its responses.

Have kids tear up the ads and throw them in the wastebasket as a symbol of rejecting smoking. (Or you could go outside and burn the ads in a safe container, letting smoking "go up in smoke.")

Close in prayer, asking God to help kids treat their bodies with respect and keep them healthy.

## ▪ Mutual Support ▪

**PURPOSE:** *to ask for God's support when it's tough to be a Christian*

**SCRIPTURE:** *1 Peter 5:8-10*

**SUPPLIES:** *Bibles, brown and red construction paper, and markers*

Have kids form two groups, and give one group red construction paper and the other group brown construction paper. Ask the "red" group members to tear their construction paper into many watermelon shapes then list on them things that are great about being a Christian. Have the "brown" group tear seed-shaped pieces of construction paper and list on them things that are tough about being a Christian.

Combine each set of partners with another pair to form small groups. Ask group members to read together 1 Peter 5:8-10 then kneel, holding hands, in a small circle. Have them pray that God's help will enable them to grow through the tough times.

Have each person grab a construction-paper watermelon or seed and take it home as a reminder that growth often comes through adversity.

## ■ A Walk in My Enemy's Shoes ■

**PURPOSE:** *to think about their enemies then pray for them*

**SCRIPTURE:** *Matthew 5:44*

**SUPPLIES:** *none*

Say: **A familiar Native American proverb says something like "Don't criticize your brother until you've walked a mile in his moccasins." Think about your enemy as I ask these questions. You may have to imagine the answer if you don't know it for certain. Don't say anything aloud; just think silently.** Ask:

● **What was your enemy's childhood like?** Pause.

● **What is it you dislike about this enemy?** Pause.

● **Why does your enemy behave this way?** Pause.

● **If you were in your enemy's shoes, how would you be similar to your enemy?** Pause.

● **How would you be different?** Pause.

● **How would your enemy be different if he or she were in your shoes?**

Close in prayer by having kids pray silently for their enemies.

## ▪ Stepping Out ▪

**PURPOSE:** *to recognize the power of prayer in reaching their goals after high school*

**SCRIPTURE:** *John 16:24*

**SUPPLIES:** *a Bible, construction paper, markers, and tape*

Give each person a sheet of construction paper and a marker. Have each one trace a foot on the paper then write on it the first step he or she will take to reach a post-high school goal. For example, someone may say, "I'll study hard right now in high school so I can graduate with honors and maybe get a scholarship for college."

Have kids talk about their steps. Tape the steps around the room as visual reminders of the steps they have to take to accomplish their goals.

Read aloud John 16:24. Say: **Let's take a moment to pray by ourselves. Ask for God's guidance with life-after-high-school goals. God promises answers to those who ask for them!**

## ▪ A Savior's Shape-Up ▪

**PURPOSE:** *to explore how God is always with them, molding their lives*

**SCRIPTURE:** *Job 10:8-12*

**SUPPLIES:** *a Bible and modeling dough*

Hand each teenager a small lump of modeling dough. Have each person shape the modeling dough to represent "a picture of me in my family." Have kids explain their shapes; for example, they may feel squeezed in, well-rounded, pulled apart, rolling along, all balled up—any feeling at all.

Read aloud Job 10:8-12. Ask:

● **What do you think Job meant?**

Pray: **Dear God, mold our lives. No matter what shape we're in right now, help us know that you are always with us and our families. You are in control, and we are never alone. Amen.**

■■■■■■■■■■■■■■■■■■■■■■■■■■■■■■■■■■■■■

## ▪ A Drug Is a Drug ▪

**PURPOSE:** *to seek God's help in avoiding drugs*

**SCRIPTURE:** *Psalm 139:13-18; Proverbs 1:10-15; Matthew 26:41; and 1 Corinthians 10:13, 28-32*

**SUPPLIES:** *a Bible, balloons, pins, and permanent markers*

Have kids form small groups. Give each group three balloons and a permanent marker. Have each group write "alcohol" on one balloon, "steroids" on another, and "marijuana" on another. Then have group members discuss the differences and similarities between the drugs. Ask:
- **How does the drug harm you physically?**
- **Why do people use (or abuse) the drug?**
- **What's the lure of the drug?**
- **How does the drug make people feel? What are the potential dangers of the drug?**

Read aloud Proverbs 1:10-15; Matthew 26:41; and 1 Corinthians 10:13, 28-32. Ask:
- **What do these Scripture passages say about temptation?**
- **How can God help you avoid the temptation to use drugs?**
- **What are better ways to feel good about yourself than using drugs?**

Read aloud Psalm 139:13-18. Say: **God loves you for who you are now—not for who you become by using drugs.**

Give each person a pin and a balloon, and reread Psalm 139:14. Have kids pop the balloons at the same time to symbolize conquering the temptation to abuse drugs.

## ▪ I'm With Ya ▪

**PURPOSE:** *to support each other in changing old ways*

**SCRIPTURE:** *2 Corinthians 3:18*

**SUPPLIES:** *paper and pencils*

Have kids form pairs, and have partners talk about ways they can support each other in changing old ways. For example, someone may say, "I'll call you once a week to see how you're doing" or "I'll start an exercise program with you." Give each person a sheet of paper and a pencil. Have partners write and sign commitments, saying specifically what they'll do.

# ▪ Partners ▪

**PURPOSE:** *to support one another in standing up for their beliefs*

**SCRIPTURE:** *Luke 21:15-19*

**SUPPLIES:** *paper*

Have kids form pairs, and give each pair a sheet of paper. Have partners take turns attempting to use only one finger to hold the sheet of paper up on its end. Ask:

● **How is this like the way you feel when you're the only one standing up for an issue?**

Then have each partner use one finger on one side of the paper to help hold it up. Ask:

● **How does this illustrate what it's like to receive help from a friend?**

● **With support from our friends and with God's help, how can we stand up for our beliefs?**

Have teenagers close in prayer while still holding up their papers, thanking God for their partners and their partners' ability to stand tall even when things get tough.

# ▪ The Fast-Food Phase ▪

**PURPOSE:** *to discuss how part-time jobs can interfere with other commitments*

**SCRIPTURE:** *Proverbs 16:3*

**SUPPLIES:** *pizza and supplies as needed for games*

Before your meeting, order out for pizza, scheduling it to arrive in time for the closing. As a closing, have kids talk about their job experiences and how jobs conflict with commitments such as school, homework, family, friends, hobbies, youth group, church, and extracurricular activities. Then pray that God will guide them in their decisions to work or not to work part time.

While you're waiting for the pizza to arrive, play zany games as takeoffs on jobs kids have. For example, have a burger-flip contest with spatulas and bean bags to see how many flips a person can make in 30 seconds. Name the winner your "burger king"!

■■■■■■■■■■■■■■■■■■■■■■■■■■■■■■■■■■■■■

## ■ Unchained Closing ■

**PURPOSE:** *to discover how to break the chains of sin*

**SCRIPTURE:** *Romans 8:1-4*

**SUPPLIES:** *a Bible, strips of paper, and tape*

Have kids form a circle. Go around the circle and "shackle" kids' hands behind their backs, using chains made from strips of paper and tape. Say: **Though we may feel bound by certain restrictions at home or at school, in Christ we're free. After I read Romans 8:1-4, celebrate your freedom by breaking your chains. Let this seal your commitment to responsibility with your freedom.**

Read aloud Romans 8:1-4 and have teenagers break their chains together.

## ■ Clique Confessions ■

**PURPOSE:** *to reflect on the damage cliques can cause*

**SCRIPTURE:** *1 Corinthians 3:1-23*

**SUPPLIES:** *candles, matches, and soft music*

Have each person take a lighted candle and stand apart from the other group members. Turn out the lights. The candlelight should look scattered. Play soft background music. Allow time for kids to quietly reflect on the times they've hurt others because of cliques.

After the personal meditation, ask individuals to go one at a time to the center of the room and offer a spoken prayer of confession for times of hurt brought on by cliques. After each member confesses, have him or her join the others to form a circle of light until everyone is together.

Say: **Jesus had a clique of sorts with his disciples. Sometimes they met by themselves, but when others were around, anyone who wanted to join was welcome. Jesus accepted everyone. The people who joined him often became members of his community.**

**That's what a church youth group really is—part of the whole body of Christ. Keeping Jesus' example in mind, let's strive to make our youth group one big, accepting, loving clique open to anyone who wants to join. We come together as one because of the light of God's forgiveness.**

Pray: **Lord, help us be more like you. Give us courage to reach** out to others and show the warmth and light of your love.

Sing or listen to a friendship song such as "Friends" by Michael W. Smith.

## ▪ Our Decision ▪

**PURPOSE:** *to overcome excuses for not going to church*

**SCRIPTURE:** *Exodus 20:8 and Acts 2:36-47*

**SUPPLIES:** *quiet music*

Ask group members to lie down in a circle with their heads facing the center. Have them close their eyes and relax. Dim the lights and play some quiet music for a few minutes. When everyone is relaxed, say: **It's Sunday morning. You've scrunched the pillow around your head to muffle your alarm clock's annoying clatter. You're not sure you want to go to church today, so you start making excuses. "Church is boring." "Nobody cares if I'm there or not." "All they want is my money." "Everybody is a hypocrite." "My faith is just between God and me." Lie there for a few moments and decide what you're going to do.**

After about one minute, ask the group members to open their eyes, stretch, and sit up. Close by saying: **Let's face it—there are numerous reasons for not going to church. The church will never be perfect. Sermons will be boring, people will speak unkind words, and the church leaders will make mistakes.**

**But don't give up. People make the church imperfect, but God can make it perfect. Accept the shortcomings and failures of the people in your church—yourself included! Focus on God's incredible love in action.**

**Ask the person on your right to pray for you. With God's support and the support of a friend, you will recognize the church in action.**

## ▪ Glorifying God ▪

**PURPOSE:** *to identify temptations and to consider if their actions glorify God*

**SCRIPTURE:** *James 1:12-15*

**SUPPLIES:** *newsprint and a marker*

Ask kids to name things that are strong temptations and list their ideas on newsprint.

Concerning each item, ask:

● **Does this glorify God?**

Encourage kids to ask that question to help them determine what is the right thing to do as they make decisions in our material world.

Close by praying: **God, help us to do everything for your glory. Help us to follow Christ's example as we live in a material world. Amen.**

## ▪ A Friendly Prayer ▪

**PURPOSE:** *to recognize the qualities of a true friend*

**SCRIPTURE:** *Proverbs 17:17*

**SUPPLIES:** *photocopies of the "A Friend Is..." handout (p. 41)*

Have kids stand in a circle and hold hands. Say: **You have nothing to lose—but everything to gain—by trying to make a friend.** Together, read aloud the "A Friend Is..." handout (p. 41) and pause after each verse. When you pause, have kids say in unison, "Thank you, God, for new friends." Close by saying "amen."

## ▪ Prevention Poster ▪

**PURPOSE:** *to close a meeting on dating or abuse by discussing ways to prevent date rape*

**SCRIPTURE:** *2 Samuel 13:10-29*

**SUPPLIES:** *tape, newsprint, and markers*

Tape a sheet of newsprint to a wall. Say: **God wants us to respect others, to love others as he loves us, and to treat people the way we want to be treated. Date rape violates God's intentions for us and our relationships. Let's brainstorm practical ways to prevent date rape.**

Give each person a marker and let kids write ideas on the newsprint. Here are some examples of ideas:

● Go out in groups.
● Date in public areas.

*(continued on p. 42)*

# A Friend Is . . .

A friend is someone who gives you time
Yet asks for no time,

Who serves
When there seems to be no reason for service,

Who is honest
When it would be easier to lie,

Who cares for you
When no one else seems to,

Who understands you
Even when you don't understand yourself,

Who accepts you for who you are
Even when others try to change you,

Who will be with you
Even when you're wrong,
Even when no one else wants to,

Who forgives you
Even when it's hard to forgive yourself,

Who trusts you
When you don't deserve to be trusted.

A friend is
Someone like you!

● Know your date extremely well.

● Don't go too far physically on a date. Cool the atmosphere before it gets hot and heavy.

● If someone you know is raped, encourage the person to talk to a counselor and work through the emotions.

Have kids gather in a circle in front of the poster. Close in prayer, asking for God's presence in kids' lives, for help in avoiding potentially dangerous situations, and for the ability to love others as Christ loves us.

# ▪ Breakout! ▪

**PURPOSE:** *to understand how racism and prejudice restrict them*

**SCRIPTURE:** *Galatians 2:11-16*

**SUPPLIES:** *a Bible and a ball of yarn*

As a group, read Galatians 2:11-16 and briefly discuss Peter's prejudice. Have kids crowd together as tightly as possible. Help kids wind a ball of yarn around and through the group until kids are completely entangled in the yarn. Ask:

● **How does prejudice entangle us and restrict us?**

● **How does prejudice affect the freedom of others?**

Say: **Peter learned from God that all people are important. When we learn that same lesson, we'll break out of the tangle of stereotyping and racism.**

Point out one thing about each person in the group that might help that person break out of the restrictions of prejudice. For example, you might say: (Name) **can break out of the entanglements of prejudice because he's so caring.** Then have kids help you get that person out of the web of yarn. When all the kids are untangled, have all the group members stand in a circle and hold hands. Close in prayer, asking God to help everyone treat other people with love and respect.

# ▪ Open Up ▪

**PURPOSE:** *to close a study on violence with a hugging exercise*

**SCRIPTURE:** *Matthew 5:38-48*

**SUPPLIES:** *none*

Have kids form two groups. Have one group stand with its arms folded. Tell kids that they must each hug three other people. Those with their arms folded have to keep them that way until they've "hugged" three other people.

When kids are finished hugging, say: **The violence in our world is like people hugging with their arms folded. Fear keeps people from opening up. Violence creates distance between us and makes it impossible for people to really care for one another. Let's pray that we can "unfold our arms" to people and stop violence around us.**

Have a group hug and close in prayer.

# ▪ I Choose ▪

**PURPOSE:** *to brainstorm reasons and ways to stay sexually pure*

**SCRIPTURE:** *Galatians 5:19*

**SUPPLIES:** *newsprint, tape, markers, index cards, and pencils*

Tape several sheets of newsprint to the wall and write, "Wall of Wisdom" at the top of each sheet. Distribute markers and have kids work together to create graffiti that describes not only why they should abstain from sex before marriage, but also ways they can protect themselves from the temptation to have sex.

When kids are finished, read kids' comments and suggestions and discuss them with the group. Ask questions such as these:

● **Is this a good idea? Why or why not?**
● **How will this idea help you abstain from sex?**
● **How can you apply this to your life?**

Give each person an index card and a pencil. Ask kids to write on their cards, "I choose to say 'yes' to abstinence until I am married" (if they're ready to make such a commitment). Then have kids sign their names on their cards and keep them as reminders of their decisions.

Say: **To help you remember your commitment, hold your left hand in front of you with the palm facing you. Notice the lines on your index finger. Pretend the lines are a continuum. The line at the base of your index finger is where a romantic relationship begins—maybe with holding hands. The last line before the tip of your finger is where you're out of control and there's no turning back. The middle line is the line you've drawn where you're** going to stop—where you're still in control and able to honor God in what you're doing. When you're in an intimate situation and things are getting heavy, look at your finger and think about where you are in relation to the line you've drawn. Muster up the courage to stop. God will be there to help you.

Have kids form a large circle, and offer a prayer, thanking God for his forgiveness when people fail to do his will. Ask for God's help in staying sexually pure and learning to avoid sexual temptation.

## • God's Wisdom •

**PURPOSE:** *to ask God for guidance in making moral decisions*

**SCRIPTURE:** *John 8:1-11*

**SUPPLIES:** *a Bible*

Read aloud John 8:1-11. Ask:
● **What moral decision did the woman make?**
● **What decision did the Pharisees want Jesus to make?**
● **What was the more important decision Jesus asked them to make?**

Say: **The woman made a wrong choice in a moral decision. But Jesus says we can't judge each other because we all make wrong choices at one time or another. Jesus forgave the woman and said, "Go and sin no more." God's grace is abundant in the story.**

Close by praying the following prayer. Pause at the end of each line and have kids silently complete each thought:

**God, help us make a moral decision to_____.**

**Forgive us for past decisions we may have goofed up on, such as_____.**

**Thank you for your grace, forgiveness, and guidance in our moral decisions. Amen.**

## • Getting Tough on Drugs •

**PURPOSE:** *to encourage teenagers to stand tough against drugs*

**SCRIPTURE:** *1 Corinthians 15:33*

**SUPPLIES:** *none*

Have teenagers scatter around the room, each one standing alone. Then have kids verbally complete the sentence you introduce.

■■■■■■■■■■■■■■■■■■■■■■■■■■■■■■■■■■■■■■■■

Say: **I can get tough on drugs alone by____.**

Then have teenagers form a large circle and hold hands.

Say: **We can get tough on drugs together by____.**

While in the circle, ask God to give each teenager the guidance and strength to fight the war against drugs.

# • "Oh, the Places You'll Go!" •

**PURPOSE:** *to explore their life goals*

**SCRIPTURE:** *Joshua 1:8-9; Jeremiah 29:11-13; Matthew 17:20; John 13:35; and Philippians 3:14*

**SUPPLIES:** *Bibles; paper; pencils; and* Oh, the Places You'll Go! *by Dr. Seuss (optional)*

Say: **A life goal is a major goal; life goals determine who you'll become. These goals are not easily achieved. To reach a life goal, a person does something each day to get closer to that goal. A person works throughout life to attain a life goal.**

One at a time, have volunteers read aloud Jeremiah 29:11-13; John 13:35; and Philippians 3:14. After each Scripture passage is read, ask kids to identify the life goal described in the Scripture. Say: **Describe a life goal you have. State the actions you take daily to reach that goal.**

Pass out sheets of paper and pencils and instruct each person to write down a life goal that is important to him or her. Encourage several kids to read their life goals aloud.

Read aloud Matthew 17:20. Ask:

● **How many of you believe you can move mountains?**

● **How are setting and reaching goals like moving mountains?**

If you have the book *Oh, the Places You'll Go!*, read it aloud. If not, continue with this activity. Ask:

● **What detours have already caused you to change your goals?**

● **How can you overcome those detours?**

Say: **In Dr. Seuss' book, he guarantees a success rate in life of 98¾ percent. God's guarantee is even stronger.**

Read aloud Joshua 1:8-9. Then pray for wisdom and strength for kids in setting and reaching their goals.

■ ■ ■ ■ ■ ■ ■ ■ ■ ■ ■ ■ ■ ■ ■ ■ ■ ■ ■ ■ ■ ■ ■ ■ ■ ■ ■ ■ ■ ■ ■ ■ ■ ■ ■ ■

# ▪ Coin Toss ▪

**PURPOSE:** *to trust God to help them make good decisions*

**SCRIPTURE:** *Proverbs 3:5*

**SUPPLIES:** *pennies*

Flip a coin. Ask:

● **Who has used this method to make a decision?**

Say: **Although we've all "tossed a coin" at one time or another, it's no way to make a solid decision. But there's something on this coin that can remind us how to make good decisions.**

Hand out pennies and let kids discover what you were referring to.

Say: **When we really trust in God and seek his will, he'll help us make good decisions. Whenever you have a big decision to make, flip a coin—not to help you make the decision, but to remind you to trust God. He'll help you make the best decision of all.**

Close with prayer, asking God to help kids make the right decisions in life.

# ▪ The Christlike Context ▪

**PURPOSE:** *to explore what is true Christian living*

**SCRIPTURE:** *Colossians 3:1-4:6*

**SUPPLIES:** *Bibles*

Say: **The Bible gives us many specific guidelines for what's right and what's wrong. But each person you meet may have a different set of guidelines. As Christians, it's our job to determine what's right and what's wrong in the context of living a Christlike life. Let's spend a few moments exploring that context silently.**

Have kids silently read and reflect on Colossians 3:1-4:6. Then have teenagers talk about what it means to live Christlike lives. Encourage teenagers to seek the right response of Christlikeness in their decisions. Close in prayer, thanking God for giving us biblical direction in choosing right from wrong.

## • Reminders •

**PURPOSE:** *to encourage kids to have patience and understanding in dealing with their parents*

**SCRIPTURE:** *Ephesians 4:32*

**SUPPLIES:** *Bibles, index cards, pens, and markers*

Have kids form small groups, and have each group read and discuss Ephesians 4:32. Give each person an index card and have him or her use markers to decorate it with the verse as a reminder to have patience during conflicts.

On the other side of their cards, have the teenagers write goals to help them better understand their parents. For example, someone may write, "I will schedule a daily talk time with my parents" or "I will ask my parents what they think about current issues." Encourage the young people to take the reminder cards home and tape them in prominent places such as on bedroom mirrors or on closet doors.

Close the session by reading this story:

**Christian comedian Ken Davis tells of a time his daughter asked to spend the night at a friend's house.**

**"No," he said.**

**"Why not?"**

**"Because I said so."**

**When Ken's wife later asked him why he said no, he replied: "Because it was only yesterday that she couldn't leave the room unless I went with her. Sometimes I say no for no other reason than because I want to know she is in the house, safe and sound and near me."**

Remind young people that parents sometimes do weird things because they love their kids so much.

## • Blending •

**PURPOSE:** *to celebrate the differences in their families*

**SCRIPTURE:** *Colossians 3:18-20*

**SUPPLIES:** *bowls, utensils, and ingredients for snack mix*

Pray: **Gracious God, you've called us together in families. Thank you for the unique people you've put into our families.**

Help us to appreciate the gifts we each have and to celebrate who we are as your children. In Jesus' name we pray, amen.

Give each group a different food that blends well with other foods; for example, an ingredient for trail mix or snack mix.

Have kids blend the ingredients and enjoy eating their blended creation.

## ▪ Pressure Prayers ▪

**PURPOSE:** *to identify pressures teens face and to pray for each other*

**SCRIPTURE:** *1 Kings 8:22-30*

**SUPPLIES:** *index cards, chairs, and pencils*

Have students sit in a circle, and give each person a pencil and an index card.

Say: **On your card, write your name and one pressure you're facing right now, such as pressure to be popular, to experiment with drugs, or to be like others.**

Have students place their cards on their chairs and stand behind their chairs. Call out a number. Have students move that many chairs to the right, silently read the cards on the chairs they stop at, and silently pray for the people who wrote on the cards. After 30 seconds, call out another number and have students again move to the right. Continue for several minutes. The last time you call out a number, have students keep the cards of the students they've prayed for. Ask kids to pray for those people this week.

## ▪ Unbreakable Bond ▪

**PURPOSE:** *to remember that nothing can separate them from God's love*

**SCRIPTURE:** *Romans 8:35-39*

**SUPPLIES:** *none*

Tell kids you need a volunteer. Have the person who volunteers stand off to one side as the rest of the kids grasp hands to form a human knot in the center of a tight circle.

Say to the volunteer: **It's your job to pull this circle completely apart. Go for it!**

The volunteer will probably start pulling on the weakest person. Kids in the circle can shift their holds to hang on to that person more securely. Even if the volunteer succeeds in pulling one person away momentarily, there's no way he or she can pull the entire circle apart.

After a couple of minutes, have the volunteer join the circle.

Say: **Just as our hands have formed an unbreakable bond, the Bible tells us that nothing can separate us from the love of God: no persecution, no mockery, no exclusion—nothing. This bond we share as brothers and sisters in Christ is a big part of the support and help God gives us.**

With the kids still hanging on to each other, have each person give thanks for the person facing him or her in the circle by finishing this sentence: "I'm glad (name of person facing him or her) is part of my support group because . . ."

Dismiss kids with this statement: **Go in God's strength and grace.**

■ ■ ■ ■ ■ ■ ■ ■ ■ ■ ■ ■ ■ ■ ■ ■ ■ ■ ■ ■ ■ ■ ■ ■ ■ ■ ■ ■ ■ ■ ■ ■ ■ ■

# High-Energy Closings

"Everything on earth, shout with joy to God! Sing
about his glory! Make his praise glorious!"
(PSALM 66:1-2).

*Most often you'll close your meeting with a reflective closing, a recap
of the day's lesson, or a prayer. But celebrative closings can be
unusual and memorable. Teenagers always love a party, a game, or something that allows them to burn off some energy. But keep in mind that
celebrations should be special—use them occasionally to catch your group
by surprise.*

## ▪ Going-Away Party ▪

**PURPOSE:** *to celebrate their upcoming journeys to heaven*

**SCRIPTURE:** *Luke 6:23*

**SUPPLIES:** *poster board, markers, confetti, and noisemakers*

Form groups of five. Give each group a sheet of poster board and
some markers. Have groups write sayings about going to heaven,
such as "Heaven Bound," "Bound for Glory," or "Upward Bound."
Encourage them to come up with original slogans. Have every
group member who's planning to go to heaven sign the poster.

Pass out confetti and noisemakers. Have kids walk around the
room, shaking each other's hands and bidding each other well, saying things such as "I'll see you in heaven. Have a good journey!"

Close in prayer, asking God to keep each person safe and stead-
fast until he or she arrives in heaven.

## ▪ Graffiti Wall ▪

**PURPOSE:** *to express what they've learned about various topics*

**SCRIPTURE:** *Proverbs 8:10 and Daniel 1:17*

**SUPPLIES:** *newsprint, tape, and markers*

Tape several large sheets of newsprint to a wall in your meeting room. Give each person a marker and tell teenagers they have two minutes to make the newsprint look like a brick wall. Then have kids write on the graffiti wall their answers to this question: "What's one thing you've learned today about (topic of your class)?" Invite them to decorate the wall with art as well.

You might want to make this an ongoing activity. Tell your teenagers that each week they'll be given time to write on the wall the key thoughts and principles from the day's lesson or to respond to what others have written by adding their own comments and questions. Remind them that no one may change or cross out what anyone else has written. However, if their personal views change throughout the course, they can alter their own graffiti to reflect those changes.

## ■ New New Year's Day ■

**PURPOSE:** *to resolve to let God plan their lives*

**SCRIPTURE:** *James 4:13-17*

**SUPPLIES:** *a Bible and refreshments*

Read aloud James 4:13-17. Ask:
● **What is the message of this Scripture?**
● **How does God feel about New Year's resolutions?**
● **What attitude would be appropriate to have in making resolutions?**

Say: **When we make New Year's resolutions, we don't know what the future will bring. And that's OK because God wants us to recognize that even when we set goals, he is the one who guides our lives.**

Form a circle and have kids close their eyes. Say: **Imagine that you're at a New Year's Eve party. The lights are bright, people are cheering all around you, the past year is behind you, and you're looking forward to the new one.** Pause. **You realize that you have to make the traditional New Year's resolution. Make your resolution silently with the attitudes that James said we should have.** Pause.

Have kids open their eyes. One at a time, have kids say, "If the Lord wills" and tell their new resolutions.

After everyone has spoken, shout: **Happy New Year!**

Close with a prayer of thanksgiving for God's direction in kids' lives.

Bring out the refreshments and celebrate the new beginnings God gives us.

## Simon Says

**PURPOSE:** *to take part in an exercise in following God's will as the Bible teaches us*

**SCRIPTURE:** *Colossians 1:1-14*

**SUPPLIES:** *none*

Have all your students stand. Say: **We're going to play a game you learned as kids. It's called Simon Says. I'll tell you certain actions to perform, but do the action only if I say, "Simon says." If I don't say, "Simon says," you should ignore the command. Those who fail to correctly follow each command must sit down.**

The faster you give the commands, the more difficult they are to follow. Use the following list as a guide. Read quickly so the students don't have time to think between commands.

Say: **Touch your toes. Simon says touch your toes and wiggle your elbows. Stop wiggling your elbows. Simon says to stand up with your hands over your head. Run in place. Do jumping jacks. Simon says stop wiggling your elbows and do jumping jacks and look over your left shoulder. Stand still. Simon says stand still and keep looking over your left shoulder. Sit on the ground. Simon says hold hands with the people next to you and do the cancan. Drop hands. Simon says everyone sit down and close your mouths.**

Say: **Even though I clearly stated what I expected from you, many of you didn't follow my directions. Why?** Ask:

● **When you're trying to follow God's will, do you sometimes feel like you did during the game?**

● **What are some ways God speaks to us?**

Say: **In the Bible, God gives us instructions for our lives. Let's remember to read and follow these instructions to help us know where God wants us to go in life.**

■ ■ ■ ■ ■ ■ ■ ■ ■ ■ ■ ■ ■ ■ ■ ■ ■ ■ ■ ■ ■ ■ ■ ■ ■ ■ ■ ■ ■ ■ ■ ■ ■ ■ ■

# ■ Resurrection Joy ■

**PURPOSE:** *to celebrate Jesus' resurrection with a group performance*

**SCRIPTURE:** *1 Thessalonians 4:14-17*

**SUPPLIES:** *photocopies of the "It's a Celebration!" handout (p. 54); whistles; and blue, red, and green construction paper*

Give each person a photocopy of the "It's a Celebration!" handout (p. 54); a whistle; and one sheet each of blue, red, and green construction paper.

Say: **We're going to celebrate Jesus' death and resurrection with this celebration responsive reading. I'll read the leader's part, and you'll read the people's part. When we come to an action, such as blowing the whistle, complete the action.**

**After we're finished, hug at least three other people and tell them each something you appreciate about them.**

After the responsive reading, join in the hugging.

# ■ Follow Everyone ■

**PURPOSE:** *to play an energetic game to end a lesson about peer pressure*

**SCRIPTURE:** *Matthew 5:10-12*

**SUPPLIES:** *none*

Play Follow the Leader with a twist. Instruct your teenagers that the first person will do an action and the second person must copy that action and add a new one. Each person must copy the actions of all the previous students and add a new action. When you reach the end of the line, have the first person in line continue, doing all the previous activities. See how long kids can remember what everyone else did.

After the activity, talk about the problems related to following the crowd. Ask:

● **When is following others too difficult or wrong?**
● **When is it best to do your own thing?**

Close with a prayer, asking God for his help and strength when teenagers deal with peer pressure.

# It's a Celebration!

*Read your part and perform the actions indicated in the parentheses.*

**Leader:** He is risen!

**People:** He is risen indeed!

**Leader:** Let everything that has breath praise the Lord.

**People:** (Blow your whistles.)

**Leader:** We have been freed to praise and serve God.

**People:** We have been freed!

**Leader:** God's love breaks all barriers.

**People:** God's love breaks all barriers.

**Leader:** Resurrection joy brings color to the drab lives of sin we once lived in.

**Leader:** Resurrection joy is in living color!

**Leader:** Then praise him with the color blue . . .

**Leader:** (Hold up your blue paper and wave it in the air.)

**Leader:** Praise him with the color red . . .

**People:** (Hold up your red paper and wave it in the air.)

**Leader:** And praise him with the color green . . .

**People:** (Hold up your green paper and wave it in the air.)

**Leader:** Praise him together like a rainbow of promise.

**People:** (Hold up all the papers and wave them in the air.)

**People:** We are the people of promise.

**Leader:** God has a surprise for us. He has changed our mourning into joy.

**People:** We will praise God with every breath in all situations.

**Leader:** Praise the Lord.

**All:** Celebrate God's love always! Amen.

## • Standing Ovations •

**PURPOSE:** *to affirm one another in a high-energy closing*

**SCRIPTURE:** *Romans 12:10*

**SUPPLIES:** *none*

As a grand finale, celebrate each person's uniqueness.

Have group members sit in a circle. Begin by announcing who will receive a standing ovation. For instance, call out "Paul." Paul must then stand and take a bow or do whatever gracious act he'd like. All the while, the other group members stand, applaud, and generally make Paul feel like a famous person they know. Then call out another person's name and repeat the standing ovation. Move on quickly so everyone gets a chance, yet move slowly enough so each person who receives an ovation can soak it all in.

## • Surprise Party •

**PURPOSE:** *to surprise your kids with a party closing, symbolizing the surprise of Jesus' resurrection*

**SCRIPTURE:** *John 20:1-20*

**SUPPLIES:** *as needed for a party*

Plan a surprise party for your teenagers. After your regular meeting, surprise them with a game- and food-filled party. Discuss how they felt about being surprised. Take a few minutes to compare their surprise with the wonderful surprise of Jesus' resurrection, and discuss its importance for us today.

## • Saying What We Mean •

**PURPOSE:** *to have fun while exploring ways people are misunderstood*

**SCRIPTURE:** *Genesis 11:7-9*

**SUPPLIES:** *newsprint and markers*

Say: **To close our meeting today, let's take a fun look at ways we can be misunderstood.**

On a sheet of newsprint, write these figures of speech:
- give me a break
- break a leg

■ ■ ■ ■ ■ ■ ■ ■ ■ ■ ■ ■ ■ ■ ■ ■ ■ ■ ■ ■ ■ ■ ■ ■ ■ ■ ■ ■ ■ ■ ■ ■

- keep your pants on
- give him a big hand
- you look like a million bucks
- chew the fat
- really came through in the clutch
- heard it through the grapevine

- drop her a line
- they had me in stitches
- knock it off
- the buck stops here
- groovy
- hold your horses

Have volunteers choose and act out these phrases as they might be understood by someone from a foreign country. Other students should guess which phrase is being acted out. Say: **It's a good thing people don't always take us literally.**

Close with prayer, thanking God for helping kids to become better communicators.

# ▪ Duck, Duck, Date ▪

**PURPOSE:** *to explore qualities they have to make dating great*

**SCRIPTURE:** *Galatians 5:22-23*

**SUPPLIES:** *newsprint, tape, and enough markers for everyone to have a different color*

Give each person a marker. In black marker, write the title "Truly Great Dates" on the top of a sheet of newsprint taped to a wall. Then list the following qualities, with three inches of space between them: love, joy, peace, patience, kindness, goodness, self-control, sense of humor, honesty, faithfulness, Christian faith (most taken from Galatians 5:22-23). Instruct each teenager to circle three qualities he or she would like future dates to have. Ask them each to underline three traits they have themselves.

Ask everyone to sit on the floor in a circle. Choose one person to be "It" and to walk around the outside of the circle, tapping each person's shoulder and saying, "Duck, duck..." When It says "date," the person It tapped chases It around the circle. If the "date" tags It, It will mention one quality he or she has that is listed on the "Truly Great Dates" list. If It makes it back to the date's spot in the circle, the date will point out one quality he or she has from the list.

Close in prayer, thanking God for great kids and asking for his guidance in their future dates.

■ ■ ■ ■ ■ ■ ■ ■ ■ ■ ■ ■ ■ ■ ■ ■ ■ ■ ■ ■ ■ ■ ■ ■ ■ ■ ■ ■ ■ ■ ■ ■ ■ ■ ■ ■ ■ ■ ■ ■ ■ ■ ■

# ▪ Potluck Party ▪

**PURPOSE:** *to teach a lesson about teamwork while creating a tasty snack to share*

**SCRIPTURE:** *Matthew 18:19-20*

**SUPPLIES:** *as needed to make a snack*

Assign each person a different ingredient from an easy-to-fix recipe to bring to the meeting, but don't tell kids what recipe their ingredients are for. At the end of the meeting, have kids work together to figure out what their ingredients make, then give them the recipe and have them make the snack. Kids will learn a lesson about teamwork and will close the meeting with a tasty snack.

Here are a couple of recipe suggestions:

## Dirt Cups
8-ounce paper cups or clear plastic cups
chocolate pudding mix
milk (as specified on pudding box)
chocolate sandwich cookies (crushed)
gummy worms

Mix the pudding according to the package directions. Layer the pudding and the cookie crumbs in cups. Top the layers with more crumbs and gummy worms.

## Peanut Butter Balls
½ cup peanut butter
½ cup honey
1 cup powdered milk
coconut
chopped nuts
sunflower seeds

Mix the peanut butter and the honey, then add the powdered milk. Knead the dough until it is smooth. Roll the dough into 1-inch balls. Pour the coconut, nuts, and seeds on wax paper and roll the balls in the mixture.

# ▪ Fix a Party ▪

**PURPOSE:** *to plan a party based on a Scriptural theme*

**SCRIPTURE:** *1 Corinthians 10:31; Philippians 4:8; 1 Thessalonians 5:16; and 2 Timothy 2:22*

**SUPPLIES:** *Bibles, party supplies, and snacks*

Have kids form four groups, and have each group read aloud 1 Corinthians 10:31; Philippians 4:8; 1 Thessalonians 5:16; and 2 Timothy 2:22. Have each group plan a party to fit the principles found in these scripture passages, such as a party to glorify God or a "pure heart" party. Call everyone back together in a large group and have the groups share party ideas, then choose one party theme, based on the biblical principles, to close your meeting.

Close in prayer, thanking God for his approval of celebrations and asking for wisdom to party in godly ways.

## • Swap-a-Sack-Lunch Picnic •

**PURPOSE:** *to enjoy fellowship as you close your meeting with a fun lunch swap*

**SCRIPTURE:** *Genesis 1:29*

**SUPPLIES:** *sack lunches and blankets*

To close your meeting with a lunch or dinner, ask each person to bring a sack lunch containing a sandwich, chips, and a piece of fruit. Allow two minutes for kids to swap sack lunches as many times as they can. The sack lunch each person is holding when you call time is the one he or she gets to eat. (Allow kids one more swap if they end up holding the sack lunches they brought to the event.) Spread out blankets in a grassy, shady area, then munch the lunches and play games if you have time.

## • Feed Me Acceptance •

**PURPOSE:** *to explore how to handle change in their lives while enjoying pizza*

**SCRIPTURE:** *2 Corinthians 3:16-18*

**SUPPLIES:** *pizza, cups, plates, napkins, and drinks*

Close your meeting by ordering enough pizza to feed your teenagers. Have kids form groups of no more than four. Divide the pizza evenly among the groups.

Say: **Accepting change is a difficult thing sometimes. Just as the disciples were often uncomfortable with the way Jesus** brought change into their lives, we often face times that are difficult to handle. During our closing today, take turns saying one thing you can do to better deal with change. After you tell an idea to your group members, each one may eat a bite of pizza. No one may eat unless someone first suggests an idea for dealing with change.

When each person has finished one piece of pizza, encourage kids to share their ideas and to chow down on the rest of the pizza.

## • Better Friend •

**PURPOSE:** *to create a puppet play based on scriptural friendship*

**SCRIPTURE:** *1 Samuel 18:1-4; 2 Kings 2:1-14; John 21:15-22; and 2 Timothy 1:1-8*

**SUPPLIES:** *Bibles, a cardboard box, scissors, markers, and white socks*

Cut a large, square hole out of a cardboard box. Have kids form groups of no more than five. Give each person a white sock and a marker. Assign each group one of the following Scripture passages to read: 1 Samuel 18:1-4; 2 Kings 2:1-14; John 21:15-22; or 2 Timothy 1:1-8.

Ask each group to write a short puppet play based on the scriptural friendship it read about. Have kids use the markers and the socks to make hand puppets. Then have each group perform its creative work for the rest of the teenagers. Use the cardboard box as a puppet stage. Close with a prayer, asking God to help your teenagers to be better friends.

## • Pass the Tie That Binds •

**PURPOSE:** *to end your meeting with a crazy contortion game*

**SCRIPTURE:** *Psalm 33:3*

**SUPPLIES:** *two neckties*

Have kids form two teams of equal size. Have each team form a line. Give a necktie to the first person in each line. Instruct teammates to pass their team's tie down the line, using their hands. Then make it more difficult—have them pass the necktie back up the line, using their elbows...then their necks...then their knees...then their ankles! Vary the relay by shouting out body-part passing instructions after every two or three passes.

It's a good idea to have a camera handy so you can preserve the laughs and strange contortions and enjoy them for months to come.

## • Top 10 List •

**PURPOSE:** *to reenact funny things that happened to the group*

**SCRIPTURE:** *Ecclesiastes 3:4*

**SUPPLIES:** *newsprint and markers*

When you have time at the end of a meeting or on a retreat, gather kids together and ask them to recall the 10 funniest things that have happened to your group. Then have kids create a David Letterman-style "Top-10 List of Hilarious Happenings." Have volunteers act out the list as it's written. Have kids decorate the list, then post it in your meeting room.

## • Praise Band •

**PURPOSE:** *to praise God with music*

**SCRIPTURE:** *1 Chronicles 15:16*

**SUPPLIES:** *a Bible, newsprint, markers, and makeshift instruments*

Read 1 Chronicles 15:16 aloud, then say: **Praise is an important part of prayer, and in the Bible, praise is often accompanied by music.**

Have kids form groups of no more than four, then give each group a sheet of newsprint and a marker. Say: **List things you want to praise God for. Then create a praise song by singing the words on your list to a familiar tune. Accompany your song with makeshift instruments; for example, run a pencil up and down a heating vent.**

After about five minutes, have each band perform its song.

## • Jesus Is... •

**PURPOSE:** *to celebrate Jesus and his teaching through parables*

**SCRIPTURE:** *Matthew 13:10-17 and parables in the Gospels*

**SUPPLIES:** *balloons and markers*

Say: **As we learn from Jesus through his teachings, we grow closer to him. Jesus' parables may challenge us to change our perspectives, but his love will always shine through even the toughest lessons.**

Give each person a balloon and a marker. Have kids blow up the balloons and write on them words describing Jesus. For example, kids might write "friend," "teacher," or "Savior."

At the same time, have kids celebrate Jesus by batting the balloons in the air and calling out the words they've written on them. Have kids continue to keep the balloons in the air and call out the words until you call out "stop!" Then allow the balloons to drop to the floor and have kids spend a moment in silent prayer, thanking God for Jesus' teachings and for his love for each person.

# Victory Cheer

**PURPOSE:** *to create a closing cheer tailored to your group*

**SCRIPTURE:** *Psalm 100:1-2*

**SUPPLIES:** *none*

This activity might become a closing ritual for your group.

Have the group make up words and actions for a special tailor-made, one-of-a-kind group cheer. Have them include rhythm claps or other cheerleading-type fun. For example, kids may say something like "Give me an F (clap, clap)! Give me a C, (clap, clap)! Give me a Y! What's that spell? First Church Youth! First Church Youth! Yea!" (Have people put their hands in the center for a huddle handshake.)

Use the cheer whenever you're ending a meeting. You might even want to lift one person onto the group members' shoulders and "carry away" a different person each week—just as in a victory celebration.

# Musical Balloons

**PURPOSE:** *to have fun with music*

**SCRIPTURE:** *Psalm 126:2*

**SUPPLIES:** *balloons*

Have everyone blow up a balloon as full as possible without tying it off. You can make a great noise with a balloon by stretching the opening of the balloon and letting a little air leak out,

■ ■ ■ ■ ■ ■ ■ ■ ■ ■ ■ ■ ■ ■ ■ ■ ■ ■ ■ ■ ■ ■ ■ ■ ■ ■ ■ ■ ■ ■ ■ ■ ■ ■ ■ ■ ■ ■ ■

vibrating the rubber as it goes. Have everyone sing "Lean on Me" or another familiar song, and have kids play along with their balloon instruments during the chorus.

## ▪ Victory Parties ▪

**PURPOSE:** *to create party themes based on Scripture*

**SCRIPTURE:** *John 20:19-31; Romans 6:1-14; and 8:31-39*

**SUPPLIES:** *Bibles, confetti, and balloons*

Have kids form two groups, and make sure each group has a Bible. Assign each group one of the following passages: Romans 6:1-14 or Romans 8:31-39. Then give both groups a supply of confetti and balloons. Say: **In your group, read the passage and discuss what implications it has for our lives today. Then create a party theme based on what you discover. In a few minutes, you'll throw a party for the other group.**

Go around and help groups find the joyful message in each passage. For the Romans 6:1-14 passage, kids might come up with the theme "victory in Christ." For the Romans 8:31-39 passage, kids might come up with the theme "more than conquerors" or "nothing can separate us from God." Encourage each group to come up with a chant or a rap describing the meaning of the group's assigned passage.

After about five minutes, have each group describe the theme of its party, do its chant or rap, and toss confetti and balloons to celebrate the message of its passage.

Then ask:

● **How did you feel as you celebrated your Scripture passage?**

● **How is that like the way we feel, knowing that Jesus overcame death?**

Say: **It's exciting to think about the impact of Jesus' victory over death. But sometimes our faith wavers as we think about who Jesus is.**

Read aloud John 20:19-31 while volunteers act out the parts of Jesus, Thomas, and the other disciples.

Then ask:

● **Have you ever felt the way Thomas did? Explain.**

● **How does the message of John 20:29 make you feel?**

Say: **Our faith is sometimes shaken by our doubts. That's** pretty normal. Yet with continued support from friends, Christian leaders, and the work of the Holy Spirit, we can grow stronger in faith.

# • "Good Egg" Friends •

**PURPOSE:** *to close your meeting with some fun games*

**SCRIPTURE:** *1 Corinthians 12:12-31*

**SUPPLIES:** *hard-boiled eggs, water, and coffee mugs*

Boil two eggs for each group member. Then have kids compete in these "eggciting" events:

● **Egg Plunge**—Have kids pair up and stand facing each other, about 10 feet apart. Give one partner in each pair a hard-boiled egg, and give the other partner a coffee mug full of water. Have the people with eggs try to toss their eggs into their partners' mugs. If a pair's egg misses the mug, that pair is out of the competition. Have pairs continue tossing eggs—standing 10 feet farther away from each other each round—until one pair remains.

● **Egg Press**—Have kids form pairs, and have pairs compete in a 50-yard dash. Call out body parts such as shoulders, hips, knees, and heads. Have each pair hold a hard-boiled egg between the specified body parts as they race. Call out a different body part after each race.

Close with a prayer, perhaps focusing on the body of Christ as described in 1 Corinthians 12:12-31.

# • Handstands for God •

**PURPOSE:** *to demonstrate that we may need help from others in standing up for God*

**SCRIPTURE:** *1 Peter 4:12-19*

**SUPPLIES:** *none*

Have kids form trios and have each person do a handstand while the other people in the trio support them.

Then say: **Sometimes it's difficult to stand up for God all by ourselves. And you may have needed extra help to do a handstand without moving. But we can depend on God to give us the help we need if we seek to follow and obey him. And we can also**

■ ■ ■ ■ ■ ■ ■ ■ ■ ■ ■ ■ ■ ■ ■ ■ ■ ■ ■ ■ ■ ■ ■ ■ ■ ■ ■ ■ ■ ■ ■ ■ ■ ■

**help one another stand when we're in tough situations.**

Have everyone form a circle, and have kids put their arms around each other. Close the session with each person praying, "God, help me stand up for you when..."

## ■ The Nose Knows ■

**PURPOSE:** *to perform a difficult exercise and discuss sticking one's nose in another person's business*

**SCRIPTURE:** *1 Thessalonians 4:11*

**SUPPLIES:** *none*

Form teams of six to eight. Have team members stand in a circle and face inward. On "go," have each person reach across the circle and grab the nose of a person who is not standing next to him or her. Have kids place their free hands behind their backs or on the wrists of the people grabbing their noses.

Tell teams to untangle their tangled hands as quickly as possible without releasing noses. If anyone in a team releases a nose, that team must start over.

End with a discussion on "being nosy" and "sticking one's nose into another's business."

## ■ Hum a Hymn ■

**PURPOSE:** *to play a guessing game with praise music*

**SCRIPTURE:** *Ephesians 5:19*

**SUPPLIES:** *hymn books or song books, small paper sacks, paper slips, and a pencil*

Prepare the small paper sacks as follows: If your hymn book has 69 hymns, for example, number seven paper slips from zero to six and place them in one sack. Number 10 paper slips from zero to nine and place them in another sack.

Have kids form two teams. Have one team pick a paper slip from each sack to form a two-digit number. The team then hums the hymn with that number in the book. For example, if a team picks a 3 and a 9, that team will hum hymn #39. If a team picks a zero and a zero, that team skips its turn.

One team member who knows the hymn can lead the rest of the

■ ■ ■ ■ ■ ■ ■ ■ ■ ■ ■ ■ ■ ■ ■ ■ ■ ■ ■ ■ ■ ■ ■ ■ ■ ■ ■ ■ ■ ■ ■ ■ ■ ■ ■

team in its attempt to hum the tune. If nobody is familiar with the hymn, let the team pick new numbers.

After the team's attempt to hum the hymn, the opposing team guesses the hymn's name. If the team guesses correctly, it scores one point. If the team's guess is incorrect, nobody scores a point. The opposing team then chooses numbers and hums a hymn. Hum along until a team wins 10 points or until your kids are all hummed out!

## ■ Surprise Ending ■

**PURPOSE:** *to celebrate Easter with a surprise party*

**SCRIPTURE:** *as selected*

**SUPPLIES:** *refreshments and music*

On or near Good Friday, hold a memorial service for Jesus, but have a surprise ending. The service should include somber songs, readings from Scripture, and dramatic testimonials from "Peter," "John," and "Mary Magdalene." Suddenly, at the end of the service, throw the doors open and have kids rush in and announce, "He's risen! Jesus is alive!" Turn on the lights, crank up the music, bring out the refreshments, and have a party. It'll be a great experience of Easter joy.

## ■ More-Than-a-Person-Can-Handle Relay ■

**PURPOSE:** *to see how much they can handle in a lesson on adultery*

**SCRIPTURE:** *Deuteronomy 5:18*

**SUPPLIES:** *a table and many small objects*

Say: **We're going to see how much you can handle in this relay. The first person will run to the table and get one object to carry back to his or her team. The second person will carry that object to the table and retrieve an additional object. Each person who follows will carry the previous objects and pick up new ones until all the objects are collected. The challenge is that you can use only one hand to pick up and carry the objects.**

Have kids run the relay, starting over when they drop items. After the race, ask:

● **How did you feel as you handled more and more items?**

Have a volunteer read aloud Deuteronomy 5:18. Ask:

● **How have our activities today helped you understand God's limitation on sexual activity as recorded in this Scripture?**

Say: **God's limitations are not to ruin our fun but to give us freedom.**

Close with prayer, thanking God for freedom that comes through observing the limits he sets.

## ▪ Friendship Charades ▪

**PURPOSE:** *to explore qualities of friendship*

**SCRIPTURE:** *Amos 3:3*

**SUPPLIES:** *paper and pencils*

Form groups of no more than six. Give each group a sheet of paper and a pencil. Ask each group to list four qualities they think are important for friendships. Then ask each group to act out those qualities without words, one at a time. Have the other groups guess the qualities.

## ▪ Potpourri ▪

**PURPOSE:** *to vary your meeting closings with memorable events*

**SCRIPTURE:** *John 14:25-26*

**SUPPLIES:** *as needed*

Here's a variety of both memorable and fun ways to end a meeting.

● Make a video for someone who just moved away.

● Host a short concert by a favorite local musician.

● Create a mural for the youth room.

● After a meeting about responding to the poor and needy in the world, send everyone out on a canned-food drive, seeing how much they can collect in half an hour.

● After a meeting in spring, make a papier-mâché egg and fill it with candy. Rent a bunny suit, go to the children's wing of a local hospital, and distribute the candy.

● Work together to fix or clean something at the church.

■ ■ ■ ■ ■ ■ ■ ■ ■ ■ ■ ■ ■ ■ ■ ■ ■ ■ ■ ■ ■ ■ ■ ■ ■ ■ ■ ■ ■ ■ ■ ■ ■ ■ ■ ■ ■ ■

# ■ Crazy Carols ■

**PURPOSE:** *to celebrate Christmas with a unique caroling party*

**SCRIPTURE:** *2 Chronicles 5:13*

**SUPPLIES:** *inexpensive musical instruments*

To close a holiday meeting with a unique Christmas caroling party, all you need are some back-up singers and inexpensive musical instruments: kazoos, slide whistles, party horns, spoons, saucepan covers, and cowbells.

Go caroling in the neighborhood of your church, surprise your Sunday school classes, visit a nursing home, or go to the mall.

A short practice session and a list of familiar songs is all you need before you go. Your group is sure to make a lasting impression!

■ ■ ■ ■ ■ ■ ■ ■ ■ ■ ■ ■ ■ ■ ■ ■ ■ ■ ■ ■ ■ ■ ■ ■ ■ ■ ■ ■ ■ ■ ■ ■ ■

# Prayerful closings

"If you believe, you will get anything you ask for in
prayer"
(MATTHEW 21:22).

*P*rayer can be a powerful way to close your meetings as teenagers seal
commitments, ask for forgiveness, worship God, express thanks, or
*intercede for others. Vary your prayer closings with leader-guided prayer,
silent prayer, and small-group prayer. Prayers can even be written letters,
poems, or songs to God. Whatever your prayer closing, know that it is
bringing your teenagers closer to God and deepening their understanding
of the power of prayer.*

## ■ Balloon Bouquet ■

**PURPOSE:** *to offer up praises on balloons*

**SCRIPTURE:** *Revelation 5:8*

**SUPPLIES:** *markers and biodegradable, helium-filled balloons*

Give each person a marker and a biodegradable, helium-filled
balloon. Read Revelation 5:8 aloud, then say: **Prayer is like sweet-
smelling incense rising up to God. Let's send up colorful
prayers of praise. On your balloon, write a sentence or draw a
picture of something you're thankful for.**

After kids finish, go outside and release the balloons all at once.
As kids release the balloons, have them say the praise they've writ-
ten. You won't hear a typical, one-at-a-time sentence prayer, but
God will hear and see a wonderful chorus of praise.

## ■ Light of the World ■

**PURPOSE:** *to hold a meditative prayer closing*

**SCRIPTURE:** *Luke 11:9-10*

**SUPPLIES:** *a candle and matches*

Have all the group members sit in a circle. Light one candle and pass it to each person in the group. Whoever has the candle says a prayer of thanksgiving, help, praise, or confession. Members have the freedom to pass the candle if they don't want to pray aloud. Encourage those who wish to pass to offer a silent prayer before giving the candle to the next person.

## ▪ Prayer Support ▪

**PURPOSE:** *to show mercy to fellow group members and to discuss how to be merciful in our lives*

**SCRIPTURE:** *Matthew 5:7*

**SUPPLIES:** *none*

Have kids form groups of no more than four. Have each person take a turn becoming "limp" while the other group members hold him or her up. Remind kids to be serious and to be careful not to drop their group members.

After groups finish, say: **Sometimes when we think about following God's example, we feel weak and unworthy. Yet God has called each of us to follow his example—as shown in Jesus—to show mercy to people in need.** Ask:

● **How is your experience with your groups like showing mercy to friends?** Allow teenagers to share responses.

Say: **Just as you held up your group members, you can support each other's efforts to be merciful in many practical ways. Sit with your group and brainstorm ways you can show mercy. Then sit silently for a minute and choose one of these merciful acts to show to someone in this group this coming week.**

After a couple minutes, close with prayer, thanking God for being just and merciful to us.

## ▪ Our Father ▪

**PURPOSE:** *to write their own versions of the Lord's Prayer, emphasizing ways God takes care of them*

**SCRIPTURE:** *Matthew 6:9-13*

**SUPPLIES:** *a Bible, paper, and pencils*

Have a volunteer read aloud Matthew 6:9-13. Say: **This prayer depicts God as our Father and describes some of the ways he** cares for his children. Find a partner and take three minutes to write your own version of this prayer, emphasizing the ways God takes care of you as your Father. We'll read these aloud as our closing prayers.

Give each pair a sheet of paper and a pencil. After a few minutes have them read aloud their prayers.

## ▪ My Tablet, My Heart ▪

**PURPOSE:** *to share a responsive prayer, asking God to help them live by his commandments*

**SCRIPTURE:** *Exodus 20:1-20*

**SUPPLIES:** *photocopies of the "Responsive Prayer" handout (p. 71)*

Have kids sit in a circle. Give each person a photocopy of the "Responsive Prayer" handout (p. 71) and ask kids to lay the prayers on the floor in front of them.

Say: **When God gave us the Ten Commandments to live by, he revealed himself to us. He revealed his love for us by giving us rules that would enable us to live life to its fullest.**

**However, we sometimes reject God by choosing to ignore and disobey his commandments.**

**Can you remember a time when you were hurt by someone you tried to love? Think of that time. Now close your eyes. Put your hands on your heart. Feel it beating? Cup your hands together, take your heart out of your chest, and hold it in your hands in front of you. There it is—your beating, sometimes hurting heart.**

Read the responsive prayer, saying the leader's part and having kids say the responses.

## ▪ I Hear You ▪

**PURPOSE:** *to pray together then take a moment of silence to listen to God*

**SCRIPTURE:** *Ephesians 6:18*

**SUPPLIES:** *none*

Have kids form pairs, and have partners take turns sharing a concern, joy, or a dream. After each partner shares, have him or her pause for a moment of silence and listen to God. Then have every-

# Responsive Prayer

**Leader:** God, please forgive us for thinking that we know better than you do the right way to live.

**Response:** God, I'm sorry for stepping on your heart when I disobey you. Forgive me, please.

**Leader:** God, as you gave Moses the Ten Commandments on stone tablets, . . .

**Response:** Write your commandments on my heart today.

**Leader:** Change our hearts.

**Response:** Give me a desire to know you and your commandments. Grant me the power to live them out.

**Leader:** God, be our guide.

**Response:** Come and guide my beating heart and fill it with your love.

**All:** Thank you, God. Amen.

one form a circle. Close with a time of silent prayer followed by a one- or two-word prayer from each teenager.

## ▪ Swords Into Plowshares ▪

**PURPOSE:** *to create sculptures that represent peace and to silently pray for peace*

**SCRIPTURE:** *Matthew 5:9*

**SUPPLIES:** *a Bible, chenille wire, paper, masking tape, scissors, and marshmallows (large or small)*

Have kids form trios. Give each trio a handful of chenille wire, a few sheets of paper, masking tape, and a handful of marshmallows (large or small). Then have each trio use these materials to create a sculpture of something that represents peace—for example, a puffy cloud or a dove. Let each group explain its sculpture, then place the sculptures around the room.

Have each teenager choose one sculpture and stand by it. Ask

■■■■■■■■■■■■■■■■■■■■■■■■■■■■■■■■■■■■■■■■■■■■

kids to close their eyes and silently pray for peace in their relationships, church, community, country, and world. Then ask them to
choose one action they'll take to help make the world less violent.
Close by reading aloud Matthew 5:9.

## ■ Stone Prayer ■

**PURPOSE:** *following a study on judging others, prejudice, or a related issue, discuss showing Christ's love to others*

**SCRIPTURE:** *John 8:7*

**SUPPLIES:** *small stones*

Give each teenager a small stone. Then read aloud Jesus' words
from John 8:7. Say: **We need to be careful not to "throw stones" at
people who are different from us or who do things we don't
approve of. Instead, we should show love to them as Jesus would.**

Have kids silently examine their stones as they consider how
they may have judged others wrongly. You might have them write
on their stones the initials of people they've judged. Ask kids to
pray silently and to ask God to guide them in their interaction with
those people.

Have kids keep the stones to remind them that everyone can be
forgiven—just as they can.

## ■ Serenity Prayer ■

**PURPOSE:** *to understand how they can follow God's will*

**SCRIPTURE:** *Matthew 12:50*

**SUPPLIES:** *photocopies of the "Serenity Prayer" handout (p. 73),
newsprint or butcher paper, tape, and markers*

Photocopy the "Serenity Prayer" handout (p. 73) and distribute
the photocopies to your teenagers. Say: **Most of us have seen the
first part of this prayer, but probably few of you have seen the
rest. It provides a good look at one man's understanding of
God's will. It may give all of us insights into how we can follow
that will.**

Read the prayer aloud together.

*(continued on p. 74)*

# Serenity Prayer

God,

grant me the serenity to

accept the things I cannot change,

courage to change the things I can, and

wisdom to know the difference,

living one day at a time,

enjoying one moment at a time,

accepting hardship as a pathway to peace,

taking as Jesus did,

this sinful world as it is,

not as I would have it,

trusting that you will

make all things right

if I surrender to your will,

so that I may be reasonably happy

in this life and supremely happy with you

forever in the next.

—Reinhold Niebuhr

■■■■■■■■■■■■■■■■■■■■■■■■■■■■■■■■■■■■

To wrap up this class, lay a large sheet of newsprint or butcher paper on the floor. Have kids trace their feet—all going the same direction—on the paper. Then have kids write in their own footprints ways they can follow God's will in their daily lives. Tape the paper to the wall as a reminder.

## ▪ Prayer of Integrity ▪

**PURPOSE:** *to pray together to do what is right*

**SCRIPTURE:** *Psalm 15*

**SUPPLIES:** *none*

Close your meeting by reading this personalized version of Psalm 15 and having kids repeat each line after you:

**Lord, how may I dwell in your sanctuary?**
**How may I live on your holy hill?**
**If my walk is blameless and I do what is righteous.**
**If I speak truth from my heart and don't slander others.**
**If I do no wrong to my neighbor and keep from saying bad things about people.**
**If I hate what an evil person does but I honor those who honor God.**
**If I keep my promises even when it hurts.**
**If I'm generous to lend money and I don't accept bribes.**
**If I do these things, I will never be shaken. Amen.**

## ▪ Receiving God's Grace ▪

**PURPOSE:** *to write letters to God, asking for his gift of grace*

**SCRIPTURE:** *Ephesians 2:5-9*

**SUPPLIES:** *paper and pencils*

Have each teenager write a letter, asking God for his gift of grace. Here is an example:

Dear God . . .

. . . when we **don't believe it,** forgive us. When we close our eyes to your free gift, open our eyes. Help us believe.

. . . when we **don't know what it is,** help us learn more about you and the grace you offer. We can draw closer to you by attending church and Sunday school, reading the Bible, and praying.

■ ■ ■ ■ ■ ■ ■ ■ ■ ■ ■ ■ ■ ■ ■ ■ ■ ■ ■ ■ ■ ■ ■ ■ ■ ■ ■ ■ ■ ■ ■ ■ ■ ■ ■ ■ ■

...when we **don't know how to get it,** help us know that grace is your free gift. Support us as we earnestly seek you every day of our lives.

...when we **don't seem to need it,** help us realize that we need your grace all the more.

Have kids form a large circle, then ask volunteers to read their letters. Place the letters in the center of the circle.

Say: **Let's think about the state of God's grace in each of our lives right now. I'll say some open-ended sentences and pause for silent prayer after each one.**

Ask kids to bow their heads as you say:

● A time in my life when I experienced God's grace was...

● An area of my life where I need God's grace right now is...

● The biggest barrier for me in accepting God's grace in this area is...

Going in order around the circle, have each person complete this sentence aloud: **God, to accept your grace right now, I need to...**

Close by praying: **God, we all sin. We all fall short of your glory. Thanks for your free gift of grace. Thanks for second chances at missed opportunities. Thanks for Jesus and his forgiveness. Amen.**

## ■ Disaster Prayers ■

**PURPOSE:** *to imagine that they have lost everything then reflect on what's really important to them*

**SCRIPTURE:** *Job 1*

**SUPPLIES:** *Bibles, a flashlight, paper, and pencils*

Have kids form groups of three, and have group members list things they'd like more of, such as clothes, friends, happiness, health, and stereo equipment.

Then have groups read Job 1.

In a dramatic tone, tell kids to close their eyes and imagine that there's been a terrible disaster—an earthquake, a hurricane, or a tornado. Everything they love, including family, friends, and possessions, has been destroyed. Only the people in this room are left. (To add to the effect, shut off the lights and turn on a flashlight.)

Distribute a sheet of paper and a pencil to each student. By the light of a flashlight, have each person list the five most important things they lost in the "disaster."

After kids reflect on what they've lost, have groups get back together to discuss their lists. Ask groups to discuss these questions:

● **Why are the things you listed so important to you?**

● **What on your list is not as important to you as you thought it was?**

● **Why do you sometimes take for granted those things that are most important to you?**

Close by having group members pray together, thanking God for blessings they take for granted.

## ▪ Living Prayer ▪

**PURPOSE:** *to sculpt themselves in prayer and to share specific prayer requests*

**SCRIPTURE:** *Matthew 21:22*

**SUPPLIES:** *none*

Have each person "sculpt" himself or herself in a prayer to God. For example, someone may lie face down on the floor or stand with arms outstretched. Have everyone pray silently for a few minutes, then have kids form pairs.

Have partners share specific prayer requests. Then have partners pray for each other while they look into each other's eyes.

## ▪ Piled-up Prayers ▪

**PURPOSE:** *to envision what it means to offer themselves as living sacrifices*

**SCRIPTURE:** *Romans 12:1*

**SUPPLIES:** *a Bible, stones, and markers*

This commitment prayer works well in an outdoor setting. Gather teenagers in a circle and give each person a marker. Read Romans 12:1 aloud. Say: **Sacrifices in Bible times were offered on altars, often made of piled-up stones. Go out and find the largest stone you can safely carry. Decide on a specific offering to make, such as a talent you can dedicate to God or an attitude you can cultivate. Then write or draw on your stone something to signify that**

■■■■■■■■■■■■■■■■■■■■■■■■■■■■■■■■■■■■■■■■■■

offering. **In 10 minutes, bring your stone back here.**

After 10 minutes, gather the group back in a circle. Then, one at a time, have them place their stones in the center of the circle to form an altar. Close by having kids pray silently for what they've written or drawn on their stones.

## ▪ Alert Prayer ▪

**PURPOSE:** *to complete an exercise about how to prepare for the end times*

**SCRIPTURE:** *Matthew 24:42-44*

**SUPPLIES:** *a Bible, index cards, pencils, newsprint, and a marker*

Have kids form groups of three or four, and give each person an index card and a pencil. Have teenagers write the reference "Matthew 24:42" on the front of each card so they know where to find Jesus' message in their Bibles. Next have them write the "ALERT" acrostic on the other side of each card. Also write the letters A, L, E, R, and T vertically down one side of a sheet of newsprint. Read aloud Matthew 24:42-44. Then ask: **What does Jesus tell us to do?**

Point to the "ALERT" acrostic and assign each group one of the letters. Say: **In your group, think of a sentence that starts with your assigned letter and that summarizes how we should be preparing for the end times.** (example: **A**ct differently, **L**ook out, **E**quip yourself, **R**ead the Bible and pray, and **T**ell others)

Have each group write its point next to its assigned letter on the newsprint, forming an acrostic. Have kids keep the cards as reminders to stay alert and ready because they don't know the day the Lord will come.

Pray: **God, help us to be alert. Help us not to worry about the end times, because you told us not to be afraid and we know that Jesus is with us forever. Amen.**

## ▪ Glad Lib ▪

**PURPOSE:** *to make Psalm 8 their own prayer of praise*

**SCRIPTURE:** *Psalm 8*

**SUPPLIES:** *a Bible, newsprint, tape, and a marker*

■ ■ ■ ■ ■ ■ ■ ■ ■ ■ ■ ■ ■ ■ ■ ■ ■ ■ ■ ■ ■ ■ ■ ■ ■ ■ ■ ■ ■ ■ ■ ■ ■ ■ ■ ■ ■ ■ ■ ■ ■

Tape two sheets of newsprint to a wall. Ask kids to name other words that mean "wonderful." Write these words on one sheet of newsprint. Then ask kids to name things God has made. Write these words on the other sheet of newsprint.

Next read Psalm 8 aloud. Pause after you read the word "wonderful" in verse 1 (New Century Version). Have kids shout out the words on the first sheet of newsprint. Then pause after you read, "I see the moon and stars" in verse 3. Have kids shout out the words on the other sheet of newsprint. When you read the last verse, pause after the word "wonderful" and have kids shout out the words on the first sheet of newsprint again.

## ■ Sounds of Silence ■

**PURPOSE:** *to set the mood for calming prayers of forgiveness*

**SCRIPTURE:** *Psalm 51*

**SUPPLIES:** *a cassette player and quiet music*

Set a mood for quiet reflection by playing calm instrumental music—no distracting lyrics. Then direct kids to pray one at a time aloud, asking for God's forgiveness for something. Tell kids they don't have to be specific about what they are asking forgiveness for in their vocal prayers. After each person prays, pause a minute for silent prayer before the next prayer is said aloud.

Pray: **God, we adore you for who you are and the great things you've done. We're sorry for the bad things we've done. Thanks for all you've given us. Amen.**

## ■ For Thine Is the Kingdom ■

**PURPOSE:** *to express love for God through the Lord's Prayer*

**SCRIPTURE:** *Matthew 6:9-13*

**SUPPLIES:** *a Bible, newsprint, markers, and tape*

Set out newsprint and markers. Have teenagers make a banner of the Lord's Prayer as a volunteer slowly reads aloud Matthew 6:9-13. Let kids take turns writing the phrases.

Have teenagers use markers to draw symbols or write words on the banner, describing their love for God. After a few minutes, tape the banner to the wall and have kids form a semicircle facing the colorful banner. Have kids hold hands, then close with a celebrative reading of the Lord's Prayer.

## • Daily Centering •

**PURPOSE:** *to focus on God in their daily lives*

**SCRIPTURE:** *Colossians 2:7*

**SUPPLIES:** *paper plates and markers*

Give each group member a paper plate and ask kids to draw concentric circles on their plates. Then have each person write, "My relationship with God" in the center of the inside circle. Ask group members to tape their plates in places where they'll see them each day. Close by squeezing everyone into a circle on the floor. Have kids offer brief prayers, asking God to help them keep their focus on him.

## • Prayer Journal •

**PURPOSE:** *to set up a prayer journal to affirm the power of prayer*

**SCRIPTURE:** *John 14:13-14*

**SUPPLIES:** *pens and a notebook or an attractively bound blank book*

At the end of each meeting, have teenagers take turns recording your group's prayer requests and praises in a notebook or an attractively bound blank book. Date each prayer-book entry. Once a month at the close of your meeting, reread what you've prayed for. Record and date the ways God has answered those prayers.

## • Prayer Connection •

**PURPOSE:** *to enhance their group's sense of community by scheduling a time each day to pray for each other*

**SCRIPTURE:** *1 Thessalonians 5:17-18*

**SUPPLIES:** *none*

At the close of your meeting, ask kids to agree on a time each school day when they all will pause for a few seconds to silently pray for each other. Have kids remind themselves of the appointed prayer time by setting their watch alarms or sticking a self-stick note to the class folders they'll be using at that time.

Kids could pray for specific needs, current world situations, or specific growth goals such as sharing their faith that day. Or kids could exchange names and each pray for a specific person in the group. Close with a group prayer, asking God to help kids keep this commitment and to answer their prayers.

## • Washed Away •

**PURPOSE:** *to identify their sins and to ask God to wash them away*

**SCRIPTURE:** *1 John 1:8-9*

**SUPPLIES:** *a Bible, washable-ink markers, a basin of warm water, a bar of soap, and a towel*

Help your kids move beyond a quickly muttered "and forgive our many sins" in their prayers of confession. Supply washable-ink markers and ask kids to write on their palms the names of sins they want washed away from their lives. Have them clench their hands tightly so no one can see what they've written.

Have kids form a circle. Bring out a basin of warm water, a bar of soap, and a towel. Say: **When you get the basin of water, say, "Jesus, please take this sin I've been hanging on to so tightly and wash it away." Use the soap to wash the writing off your hand, then dry it with the towel. Pass the supplies to the next person.**

Close by having kids put their clean hands, palms up, into the circle. Ask a volunteer to read 1 John 1:8-9 aloud.

## • Prayer With a Beat •

**PURPOSE:** *to "pray" by listening to Christian music*

**SCRIPTURE:** *Psalm 150*

**SUPPLIES:** *a cassette player or a CD player and music by Christian artists*

Many contemporary Christian songs are prayers, such as songs that use the word "you" when referring to God. Ask kids to listen to their favorite Christian artists, such as Amy Grant or Michael W. Smith, for songs that are addressed directly to God. Then have kids bring their favorite songs to your next meeting. (Provide cassette tapes or compact discs for kids who don't listen to Christian music on their own.)

Don't discuss or dissect the songs; just play them and listen, letting the songs' words become your group's prayers. Your kids will see that prayer can be expressed in ways they enjoy, not just in "churchy" phrases.

For extra fun, give kids paper and colored markers (or bright tempera paints and paintbrushes). Play a song and have kids "draw" the song as they listen. Hang the prayer posters on the wall in the meeting room.

# ■ Power-Walking ■

**PURPOSE:** *to experience the power of prayer*

**SCRIPTURE:** *Luke 11:9-10*

**SUPPLIES:** *none*

Every few months, you might want to close your meeting with a prayer walk. Here's how to get the full impact of a prayer walk:

**P**reliminaries—Have kids form groups of no more than four. Choose an area and set aside enough time for the walk so you aren't rushed. Determine the route your groups will take. If you make this a regular event, recruit Christians of all ages to join your prayer-walking groups.

**R**esearch—Find out all you can about the area and the people you'll be praying for: Have these people encountered any significant problems? What's unique about this area's history? Ask the Holy Spirit to give you insight into the people's spiritual and physical needs. Let people know that you'll be coming through to pray for them. Ask for specific requests they'd like you to pray for.

**A**rea—When you walk through an area, personalize your prayers to people's needs. Pray aloud for families, teachers, students, employees, and church members.

**Y**our focus—Keep your focus on God. Don't be discouraged by the magnitude of the problems. Remember how big our God is!

**E**ffect—Prayer changes things. Thank God ahead of time for his ability to change people's lives and circumstances.

**R**egroup—After each prayer walk, meet together so everyone can talk about the experience. Follow up the prayer walk by discovering any answers to prayer.

# • Timeout to Listen •

**PURPOSE:** *to take time out to listen to God*

**SCRIPTURE:** *Ezekiel 33:30-32*

**SUPPLIES:** *cupcakes, matches, and a birthday candle*

Say: **God's voice can get crowded out by all the stuff that fills our lives. That's why it's important to take some time out.**

**You can take time out for God by**

● **praying,**

● **stopping and listening after you pray to hear if God has anything to say, or**

● **taking a long walk and imagining that Christ walks with you.**

**For example, imagine what Jesus is saying to you. Or imagine that he's simply walking with you in loving silence.**

**Learning to listen to your heart as well as your head is the first step in hearing God's voice in your life.**

Place a cupcake with a birthday candle in it on the floor. Gather kids in a circle around it. Turn out the lights and light the candle. Have kids take time to pray then listen for God's answers while the candle burns. When the candle burns down to the cupcake, close with prayer, asking God to help the kids take time to listen to him through prayer, the Bible, and their hearts. Serve cupcakes to close your meeting.

# • When You Pray... •

**PURPOSE:** *to learn how to communicate with God through prayer*

**SCRIPTURE:** *Matthew 6:9-13 and Luke 11:5-13*

**SUPPLIES:** *a photocopy of the "Performance" handout (p. 84)*

Before the meeting, read the "Performance" handout (p. 84) at least once to become familiar with it. Also select one volunteer to lead the pantomime actions, and give him or her a photocopy of the handout. Encourage your volunteer to read the skit beforehand and to practice the motions. Use this skit to close your meeting.

Say: **Imagine what life would be like if no one could pray. Knowing that God had the power to work miracles and yet not being able to communicate with God would be frustrating, confusing, and unbearable.**

■ ■ ■ ■ ■ ■ ■ ■ ■ ■ ■ ■ ■ ■ ■ ■ ■ ■ ■ ■ ■ ■ ■ ■ ■ ■ ■ ■ ■ ■ ■ ■ ■ ■ ■ ■ ■ ■ ■

Many teenagers face the prospect of prayer with similar feelings. They don't know how to talk to God and aren't sure that God wants to hear what they have to say. As a result, many frustrated and confused teenagers simply give up on prayer.

Let's use this skit to help us overcome negative feelings about prayer by learning how to communicate with our heavenly Father.

Have the group stand, facing you and your volunteer. Inform kids that they will perform an echo-pantomime based on Matthew 6:9-13. Ask students to act out what you say by mimicking the volunteer's pantomime actions. They won't need copies of the handout.

Tell kids this skit should be performed in complete silence. Then read the skit with feeling and at a steady pace. Be sure to allow enough time for students to mimic the volunteer and to feel the emotion of the skit.

If you want a longer closing activity, have kids read Matthew 6:9-13 and Luke 11:5-13 and discuss these questions.

● How did you feel during the skit? How do you feel when you pray?

● How would you define "prayer"? Why should people pray? What kinds of things should be included in prayer?

● What about prayer is hard for you? How can you overcome those obstacles?

For further study, have kids form four groups and give each group a map of the world. Have groups brainstorm needs that people might have in different parts of the world, then lead kids in praying for those needs.

## ■ Prayer Power ■

**PURPOSE:** *to ask God to respond to individual prayer requests*

**SCRIPTURE:** *Psalm 70*

**SUPPLIES:** *a Bible, index cards, and pencils*

Say: **The Bible describes the power of prayer. Let's put that power to use!**

Give each person two index cards and a pencil. Say: **On each card write one specific area of your life that could be affected by the power of prayer; for example, you might write, "I don't know any Christians at school, and I'd like God to let me meet some" or "There's a lot of tension in my home, and I'd like God to help**

*(continued on p. 85)*

# The Performance

| The Script | The Actions |
|---|---|
| In this manner, therefore, pray: | *Fold hands and bow head.* |
| Our Father | *Raise hands and look up in praise.* |
| in heaven, | *Point up and swirl hands in the air to suggest clouds.* |
| hallowed be Your name. | *Raise arms and bow from the waist.* |
| Your kingdom come. | *Make sweeping motion with one arm.* |
| Your will be done | *Point up, hit fists together, and outstretch hands with palms up.* |
| on earth | *Touch the ground with one finger.* |
| as it is in heaven. | *Point up and swirl hands in the air to suggest clouds.* |
| Give us this day | *Cup hands together to form a bowl.* |
| our daily bread. | *Make eating motions.* |
| And forgive us our debts, | *Look up and wring hands.* |
| as we forgive our debtors. | *Stretch out arms forward with palms up.* |
| And do not lead us into temptation, | *Cover eyes with hands.* |
| but deliver us from the evil one. | *Hide face in hands and crouch in fear.* |
| For Yours | *Raise arms high in praise.* |
| is the kingdom | *Sweep out with both arms, palms up.* |
| and the power | *Swirl hands in circles as you raise arms high.* |
| and the glory | *Applaud.* |
| forever. | *Make sweeping motion with right arm.* |
| Amen. | *Kneel on one knee. Fold hands and bow head.* |

(Matthew 6:9-13, New King James Version)

my family get along." You can put your name on the cards if you want, but you don't have to.

Place more cards around the room so kids can take as many as they want.

When everyone is finished, collect the cards. Have teenagers form groups of no more than three. Then give each group several cards.

Say: **Read aloud these prayer requests together and pray for the people who wrote them, whether or not you know who they are. Ask God to enter each situation and to respond with power and compassion.**

Allow as much time as it takes for kids to pray for each request. If you prefer, keep the prayer time moving quickly by passing cards from group to group.

Close the meeting by reading aloud Psalm 70.

Be sure to follow up on the answers to prayer over the following weeks.

## ▪ Binding Promises ▪

**PURPOSE:** *to pray for strength in pursuing future goals or dreams*

**SCRIPTURE:** *Isaiah 12:2*

**SUPPLIES:** *cloth strips*

Say: **Let's commit our dreams to God and trust him to give us strength to pursue our dreams.**

Form pairs. Have partners take turns saying, "I trust God to give me strength to pursue my dream of . . . " Have partners help each other tie a cloth strip to one of their wrists as a symbol of their commitment.

As a large group, join hands and pray for God to give kids strength and courage to make their dreams reality.

## ▪ A Discipline of Silence ▪

**PURPOSE:** *to encourage meditative prayer*

**SCRIPTURE:** *Matthew 6:6*

**SUPPLIES:** *a Bible*

This type of closing can be effective in helping kids get serious about their relationships with God. For an extended period of time (from 10 minutes to 20 minutes), no one is allowed to speak.

Instead, everyone spends time in reflection, meditation, or prayer.

To help kids focus, read an appropriate Scripture passage to get them started. Read a passage about prayer or a passage that relates to your meeting topic. You may want to read another Scripture passage halfway through the meditation time.

## ▪ Biblical Hypocrites ▪

**PURPOSE:** *to understand how to be true to themselves*

**SCRIPTURE:** *Matthew 23:1-36*

**SUPPLIES:** *Bibles, paper plates, markers, tape, and craft sticks*

Give each person two paper plates, markers, tape, and craft sticks. Ask each person to create two different masks with these supplies. One mask should represent a Christian attitude. The other mask should represent a non-Christian attitude. Have kids form small groups and read aloud Matthew 23:1-36. Have group members identify the Pharisees' hypocritical actions. Ask:

● **Why was Jesus so upset with the Pharisees?**

● **What was Jesus' message to the Pharisees?**

Ask group members to take their masks and to each find a quiet place in the room. Have them take a moment to reflect on times when they've acted the way the Pharisees did. Ask them to pray silently for strength to be true to God—both inwardly and outwardly.

Have kids form a circle. Ask each person to hold both masks in front of his or her face. Have group members take turns saying, "Lord, help me be true to you and myself...always" as they take down their masks and throw them into the center of the circle. After the last mask is tossed, close with a group hug.

## ▪ Manly and Womanly Prayers ▪

**PURPOSE:** *to pray that the guys and girls in their group will develop good qualities as husbands and wives*

**SCRIPTURE:** *Proverbs 31:10-31 and 1 Timothy 6:11-21*

**SUPPLIES:** *none*

Have the girls in your group form a circle around the guys and name characteristics of good husbands or boyfriends. Have each girl choose a characteristic and pray for that characteristic to grow in each guy's life.

Then have the guys in your group form a circle around the girls. Have guys name characteristics of good wives or girlfriends. Have each guy choose a characteristic and pray for God to develop that quality in each girl.

## ▪ World Prayers ▪

**PURPOSE:** *to identify and pray for people in other countries who need God's help*

**SCRIPTURE:** *Luke 18:1-8*

**SUPPLIES:** *newspapers*

Using a newspaper as a guide, have kids pick out five countries whose people need God's help with specific problems. Then have kids break into five groups and spend a few minutes praying for their assigned countries' specific needs.

## ▪ Prayer Chain ▪

**PURPOSE:** *to identify prayer requests and to make a paper chain of their requests*

**SCRIPTURE:** *Matthew 21:22*

**SUPPLIES:** *1×6-inch paper strips, pencils, and tape*

Give each person a 1×6-inch paper strip and a pencil. Say: **Prayer is our connection with God. Take a moment to consider what you'd like to talk with God about. You may have a concern you'd like to pray for or a joy you'd like to thank God for.**

Have kids write on each slip a prayer request or something they're thankful for. For example, kids might express concerns about family situations or joy about things that are going well.

Have a volunteer read aloud his or her strip then tape the ends together to make a paper chain link. As kids read aloud their prayer requests, have them add their strips to the previous links to form a "prayer chain." Connect the ends of the chain together to form a complete circle with the paper links.

Have kids form a circle. In closing, pass the prayer chain around the circle and have each person offer a silent prayer as he or she holds the chain. Hang the chain in your meeting room and add to it as desired at future meetings.

# Servanthood Closings

"The servant does not get any special thanks for
doing what his master commanded"
(LUKE 17:9).

*T*eenagers often seem self-centered, but give them the opportunity to help someone else and, with your direction and ideas,
*they'll often jump at the chance. If you model and teach servanthood
to your teenagers, they'll feel good about themselves and they will live
their Christianity by serving others.*

## ■ Forever and Ever, Amen! ■

**PURPOSE:** *to ask God for strength in serving others*

**SCRIPTURE:** *Matthew 28:20*

**SUPPLIES:** *a Bible*

Ask kids what infinity means (endless, unlimited). Say: **The infinity symbol is a figure-eight. Let's form a figure-eight and join
hands.**

**Jesus' love is endless. He is ready to serve us, providing never-
ending encouragement and strength as we serve others.**

Go around the figure-eight and let each person share a way he or
she can personally serve someone else this week. Close in prayer,
asking for God's help to serve others and thanking God for his ever-
lasting encouragement and love. Read Matthew 28:20 as an "amen."

## ■ Cleanup Closing ■

**PURPOSE:** *to serve their community by having a challenging cleanup*

**SCRIPTURE:** *Genesis 2:15*

**SUPPLIES:** *trash bags and a litter list*

Have a "litter-al scavenger hunt." Challenge kids to "bag" typical
objects that litter your city or town's streets. Give each person a

trash bag, your litter list, and a time limit. It's a great way to clean up your community and keep God's creation beautiful!

## • Your Serve! •

**PURPOSE:** *to brainstorm ways they can serve others then to "serve-up" their ideas*

**SCRIPTURE:** *Matthew 20:25-28*

**SUPPLIES:** *a Bible, a badminton racket, a birdie or a volleyball or basketball, and a trash can*

Have someone read Matthew 20:25-28. Ask:

● **What does Jesus tell us about servanthood?**

After students respond, say: **Jesus commissions us to serve others, but he practices what he preaches. How are we going to practice what Jesus preaches?**

Have each person present a serve-solution then try to "serve" the badminton birdie (or the volleyball or basketball) into the trash can. Each time a person scores a goal, have everyone yell, "Great serve!" Make it easier by having everyone stand around the trash can and help the birdie or the ball into the goal.

Ask kids to form a circle around the trash can. Close with a prayer, asking for God's help in serving others.

## • Wrap It Up •

**PURPOSE:** *to affirm each other as servants*

**SCRIPTURE:** *Galatians 5:13*

**SUPPLIES:** *newsprint, tape, markers, and gift bows*

Tape three sheets of newsprint to the wall. Label the sheets "family," "friends," and "others." Give each person a marker. Have kids write on the newsprint ways they can serve these people in the coming week. Afterward have a volunteer read aloud the ideas on each sheet.

Then tape a gift bow on each person as you say, "You are a gift."

Close in prayer, asking God to help kids find God's joy in giving themselves away.

■■■■■■■■■■■■■■■■■■■■■■■■■■■■■■■■■■■■■

## ▪ Beyond Sacrifice ▪

**PURPOSE:** *to find joy in serving others*

**SCRIPTURE:** *John 13:1-17*

**SUPPLIES:** *none*

Say: **If we think only about the pain or sacrifice involved in serving, we're missing the best part. Beyond sacrifice is the incredible
joy of knowing you're doing God's work in the world. And that joy
makes even the most painful serving action feel good.**

Have kids stand in a circle facing inward, then have them turn
sideways to face right. On "go," have kids serve each other by each
giving the person in front of them a back rub. After a minute, call
time and close in prayer, thanking God for sending Jesus as an
example of the kind of servant we should strive to be.

## ▪ Group Givers ▪

**PURPOSE:** *to find ways to serve those less fortunate than themselves*

**SCRIPTURE:** *Matthew 25:31-46*

**SUPPLIES:** *Bibles, newsprint, markers, and tape*

Have kids form groups of no more than three. Give each group a
Bible, a sheet of newsprint, a marker, and one of the following
descriptions: "hungry or thirsty," "alone or without clothes," or "sick
or in prison." It's OK if more than one group is assigned the same
description. Have each group appoint a reader who will read
Matthew 25:31-46, a recorder who will write ideas on the newsprint,
and a reporter who will tell the ideas to the rest of the class.

Have groups identify actual people in their communities who fit
their descriptions and list ways to serve these people. For example,
they may list, "poor or unemployed people—collect canned and pack-
aged food for them"; "homeless people—collect money and clothing
for them"; or "people in nursing homes, hospitals, and prisons—send
cards and letters to them."

After several minutes, have each group's reporter share the
group's ideas. Tape the newsprint lists on a wall.

Have your teenagers select one "giver" idea from the newsprint
lists that they can plan right now. For example, they can plan to
collect clothing for the homeless.

Have kids brainstorm the steps needed to accomplish the task then plan to carry them out at a future meeting. For example, have kids form three groups. Have one group write an announcement for your church bulletin and newsletter, saying your youth group is sponsoring a clothing drive for the homeless. In the announcement, tell congregation members what date they should bring blankets, coats, gloves, pants, shirts, and socks to church.

Have another group search the church for boxes they can decorate to hold the collected clothing.

Have another group design posters to place by the boxes. One poster may include details of the clothing drive. The other poster might be a note from Jesus that says, "What you do for the least of these, you also do for me. Love, Jesus."

## ▪ Serving Ways ▪

**PURPOSE:** *to practice servanthood in their families*

**SCRIPTURE:** *Mark 10:35-45*

**SUPPLIES:** *newsprint, a marker, tape, index cards, and pencils*

Tape a sheet of newsprint to the wall. Have kids brainstorm ways to serve their friends and family members and write these on the newsprint. Encourage kids to be creative. For example, someone might say, "Cook a meal for your family," "Do a friend's chores for a day," or "Organize your family photos."

Give an index card and a pencil to each student. Have each person pick one idea from the list to do during the week. Have each person write his or her idea and name on the index card. Collect the cards. Close by saying: **Next week, we'll briefly review the cards to see how you did in following through on your plan to serve.**

Remember to save the cards and review them at your next meeting.

## ▪ Operation Reach Out ▪

**PURPOSE:** *to reach out to someone on the way home from your meeting*

**SCRIPTURE:** *Matthew 25:31-46*

**SUPPLIES:** *photocopies of the "Operation Reach Out" handout (p. 93) and transportation*

■ ■ ■ ■ ■ ■ ■ ■ ■ ■ ■ ■ ■ ■ ■ ■ ■ ■ ■ ■ ■ ■ ■ ■ ■ ■ ■ ■ ■ ■ ■ ■ ■ ■ ■ ■ ■ ■ ■ ■

Kids will give away good feelings with this service project.

Ask several adult drivers to help. Have kids form groups of four or fewer, and assign each group an adult driver. Give each group a photocopy of the "Operation Reach Out" handout (p. 93).

Have groups read Matthew 25:31-46, then have each group choose one "reach out" activity to do on the way home from your meeting. At the beginning of your next meeting, have them share what they did.

# ▪ Sands of Time ▪

**PURPOSE:** *to brighten the day of a shut-in with a telephone call*

**SCRIPTURE:** *Philippians 2:1-4*

**SUPPLIES:** *names and telephone numbers of shut-ins from your congregation or in your community*

Close your meeting by giving each person the names and telephone numbers of two shut-ins from your congregation or community. Say: **Every other day, call your assigned friends and visit with them for at least three minutes. Identify yourselves, ask questions about them, and tell them about yourselves.**

During future youth group meetings, ask kids to tell about their conversations. Affirm kids' attempts to reach out to others.

# ▪ Good Servants ▪

**PURPOSE:** *to give of themselves to help those in need*

**SCRIPTURE:** *Ecclesiastes 11:9*

**SUPPLIES:** *none*

You may want to end a meeting on servanthood by giving kids specific tasks to carry out during the week. At the next meeting, be sure to check on how they did.

Kids could

● interview grandparents or parents about what life was like when they were teenagers,

● help older people or disabled people in the neighborhood with housework,

● tutor kids who are struggling in certain subjects, or

● explain their faith to friends.

# Operation Reach Out

**1.** Go to a grocery store, buy a flower, and give it to the cashier. Say, "God bless you and have a good day!"

_____
signature

_____
location

_____
driver's signature

**2.** Help two people carry their groceries to their cars.

_____
signature

_____
location

_____
driver's signature

**3.** Give a total stranger a sincere compliment.

_____
signature

_____
location

_____
driver's signature

**4.** Create your own blessing. Write the idea here:_____

_____.

_____
signature

_____
location

_____
driver's signature

# ■ Winter Outdoor Outreach ■

**PURPOSE:** *to serve others in their community with small acts of kindness*

**SCRIPTURE:** *2 Corinthians 6:6*

**SUPPLIES:** *as determined*

Try this creative closing to serve people in the midst of winter. Ask a local supermarket for permission to de-ice and clean the windshields of customers' cars. Use cans of de-icer and dry cloths to make the windshields clear. (If you live in a warmer climate, clean the windshields with glass cleaner.) On each car, leave a note that reads, "The _____ youth group cleaned your windshield as a way to show you God's love. Have a nice day!"

# ■ Servant Day ■

**PURPOSE:** *to happily serve their families*

**SCRIPTURE:** *Mark 10:43-45*

**SUPPLIES:** *none*

Have each teenager choose a day to become a servant for his or her family. Kids should tell their parents that they're doing this as a way of saying, "I love you." Have kids complete tasks that their parents assign—tasks that go beyond their daily required chores. Parents can give each teenager a list of chores such as washing dishes, doing the laundry, ironing, doing yardwork, shopping for groceries, washing the cars, or driving younger siblings to activities.

At the next youth meeting, have teenagers tell about their experiences and their feelings about their servant day. Have kids write letters to their parents, thanking them for the hard work they do as parents.

# Thoughtful Closings

"Think only about the things in heaven, not the things on earth"
(COLOSSIANS 3:2).

*As teenagers learn about Christianity, they have many questions about concepts such as faith, salvation, and grace. Closing your meetings with thoughtful discussions and prayers can help them understand these concepts and put them into practice in their lives. Thoughtful closings often leave lasting impressions of your meetings.*

## ▪ "One Way" Celebration ▪

**PURPOSE:** *to explore how Christianity has made a difference in their lives*

**SCRIPTURE:** *2 Corinthians 5:20*

**SUPPLIES:** *paper and markers*

Say: **The more we see how our faith makes a difference in our lives, the more we can be assured that the Christian faith is the only true way to get to heaven. Let's express our faith in a "one way" celebration.**

Give each teenager a sheet of paper and a marker. Have each person draw a large arrow on his or her paper and write, "One Way!" at the top. Then have everyone write one way that Christianity has made a difference in his or her life.

After a minute, have volunteers tell what they wrote. Say: **Because Christ lives in each of us, we all can help each other see Christ in our daily lives. Write on each person's sheet one way you see Christ in him or her.**

Allow several minutes for kids to mingle and write on all the sheets. When everyone is finished, have kids form a circle and close with this prayer: **Dear Jesus, give us the wisdom and insight to see the truth of our Christian faith, and help us reach out to those in other religions and share with them the message of Christ. In Jesus' name, amen.**

## ▪ For God ▪

**PURPOSE:** *to recognize the suffering they might endure in keeping their commitments to God*

**SCRIPTURE:** *Romans 5:3-5*

**SUPPLIES:** *a Bible, index cards, and pencils*

Read aloud Romans 5:3-5 to your group.

Give each person an index card and a pencil. Say: **On one side of your card, write the quality from Romans 5:3-5 that you would most like to possess. On the other side, write your commitment to God to endure suffering for him.**

Encourage kids to take the cards home and post them where they'll see them daily. Close by thanking God for the ways kids will benefit from the suffering they'll go through in living for him.

## ▪ Imagine ▪

**PURPOSE:** *to imagine that they witness Jesus' return*

**SCRIPTURE:** *1 Thessalonians 4:13-18*

**SUPPLIES:** *none*

Have kids sit on the floor and close their eyes. Tell them to imagine that the following story is happening to them. Pause after each question to give kids time to reflect.

Read this story: **One day while walking down the street, you see a crowd gathering. You hear the people saying something about "coming from the skies." What do you think about?** Pause. **You inch your way through the crowd to where you can see the back of someone who seems almost radiant. He turns around and looks into your eyes. It's Jesus! How do you feel?** Pause. **What does he say to you?** Pause. **Keep your eyes closed and imagine this scene. I'll call time after two minutes.**

After two minutes, have kids tell what they felt. Then close in prayer, asking God to help kids face the end times with hope and courage.

## ▪ Giant Slayers ▪

**PURPOSE:** *to learn that with God's help they can handle their fears*

**SCRIPTURE:** *1 Samuel 17:45 and Psalm 18:2-3*

**SUPPLIES:** *a Bible; markers; and small, smooth stones*

Read aloud David's words to Goliath from 1 Samuel 17:45.

Say: **The power of God can remove fears from your life, too. Just remember David and who he trusted to help him overcome his fears.**

Give each teenager a marker and a small, smooth stone.

Read aloud Psalm 18:2-3. Then have kids write, "Psalm 18:2-3" on their stones. Urge them to keep their stones handy to remind them how to handle fears.

# ▪ Trust and Relax ▪

**PURPOSE:** *to relax and feel God's peace*

**SCRIPTURE:** *Philippians 4:6-7*

**SUPPLIES:** *a Bible and a chalkboard and chalk (or newsprint and markers)*

Have a volunteer read aloud Philippians 4:6-7. Ask for paraphrases of the passage, and write them on a chalkboard or newsprint. Say: **Relax and let God's promise of peace become real to you.**

Have partners sit back-to-back and lean against each other. Then have kids close their eyes and imagine themselves standing under a cool, refreshing waterfall in a tropical paradise. Say: **The water is the peace of God flowing down into every area of your life, washing all worry and tension away.**

While kids think about this, slowly read aloud Philippians 4:7 three times. Then offer a brief benediction of peace to close the meeting, such as "God's peace be with you."

# ▪ A Gift of Grace ▪

**PURPOSE:** *to open themselves to accepting God's grace*

**SCRIPTURE:** *Ephesians 2:6-9*

**SUPPLIES:** *none*

Have kids form groups of no more than three. Have kids discuss the following question:

● **If you knew you were going to be given straight A's at school** no matter what the quality of your work (or even if you never attended), how would that change the way you approached school?

Ask teenagers to discuss how this scenario is similar to the way we approach God's grace. Encourage kids to speak honestly about their struggles with accepting God's gift of love and the promise of eternal life. Then ask:

● **What does it mean to walk in grace?**

● **How do our mistakes affect our relationship with God?**

● **How would our relationship with God be different without grace?**

Say: **God's grace is an undeserved, incredible expression of his love for us. But too often we get caught up in trying to get closer to God through our actions instead of living in humble awe of God's love.**

Have volunteers close the meeting by thanking God for his gift of grace. To help kids remember God's grace, encourage them to say the word "grace" every time they eat a meal or a snack during the coming week. As they say the word, have kids think about God's grace and thank him for demonstrating what true love is all about.

## ■ Rewards of Commitment ■

**PURPOSE:** *to discuss God's promised reward of an eternity in heaven*

**SCRIPTURE:** *Matthew 16:27 and 28:20*

**SUPPLIES:** *Bibles and treats such as candy or fruit*

Ask two volunteers to read aloud Matthew 16:27 and 28:20. Ask:

● **What is the reward for committing our lives to Jesus?**

● **Is it worth the commitment? Why or why not?**

Hand out treats such as candy or fruit. Say: **This is your reward for your commitment in attending this meeting.** Ask:

● **How did it feel to receive a reward?**

● **How is this like the reward for committing yourself to be Jesus' disciple?**

Say: **Jesus never promised that being his disciple would be easy. But he did promise to always be with us. And he promised us the reward of an eternity in heaven. That's pretty tough to beat.** Close with a prayer, thanking God for always being with us and for his promise of an eternity in heaven.

# • Questions for God •

**PURPOSE:** *to learn to trust in God, who knows everything*

**SCRIPTURE:** *Isaiah 48:3-5*

**SUPPLIES:** *paper, pencils, and a basket*

Give a sheet of paper and a pencil to each student.

Say: **We all have questions we want to ask God someday. Is there another planet like Earth in the universe? Why are there so many different races and cultures of people with so many languages, and why can't we all get along? Can animals communicate with one another? Write one question for your Creator and put it in this basket.**

Pick each question at random and read it aloud. Have kids ponder and discuss the questions but rather than try to answer them, trust that God knows the answers.

# • The Best Gift •

**PURPOSE:** *to brainstorm creative ways to show appreciation to their parents on Father's Day or Mother's Day*

**SCRIPTURE:** *Exodus 20:12*

**SUPPLIES:** *pens, envelopes, and paper*

Have kids form groups of no more than three. Have teenagers tell about Father's Day gifts their fathers really liked (or adjust accordingly for Mother's Day). Have kids brainstorm creative ways to thank their fathers for "just being dad." Each group should report its ideas to the other groups. Then invite kids to vote on the "best" idea and commit to carry out the winning idea for their dads. Have kids who don't have fathers at home choose and show their appreciation to adults they respect.

Distribute a pen, two sheets of paper, and two envelopes to each person. Ask everyone to write a brief letter of thanks to God for being the ultimate father. Then have kids who feel comfortable doing so write similar letters to their earthly fathers. Encourage kids to keep the letters to God as reminders of God's love for them. Have kids deliver or mail their letters to their dads.

■■■■■■■■■■■■■■■■■■■■■■■■■■■■■■■■■■■

# ▪ Letter to Myself ▪

**PURPOSE:** *to identify what kinds of people they'd like to be in a year*

**SCRIPTURE:** *Romans 12:1-2*

**SUPPLIES:** *a Bible, paper, pencils, and envelopes*

Read aloud Romans 12:1-2. Give each person a sheet of paper, a pencil, and an envelope. Ask kids to think about the kinds of people they'd like to be in a year, based on the Scripture. Have each one write himself or herself a letter describing that person. Ask volunteers to tell what they wrote, then have kids seal their letters in the envelopes. On the envelopes, have kids write their names and "to be opened on (date one year from now)." Encourage kids to keep the letters in their Bibles so they won't misplace them before it's time to open them.

Have kids form a circle and offer short prayers, asking God to reveal his will for their lives—for what they're to do and who they're to become.

# ▪ Resurrection Revelry ▪

**PURPOSE:** *to celebrate Christ's resurrection*

**SCRIPTURE:** *John 20:1-20*

**SUPPLIES:** *fruit, cups, and juice*

Close your meeting by serving fruit and juice to your group. Have kids tell stories about things in their lives that have gone through "death" only to be resurrected. For example, someone might tell about a class he or she was failing but passed by the end of the school year or about a relationship that was "dead" then was rekindled.

Close the celebration with prayer, thanking God for sending Jesus.

# ▪ Legacy Closing ▪

**PURPOSE:** *to record the blessings in their lives as journal legacies for their families*

**SCRIPTURE:** *Proverbs 3:1-2*

**SUPPLIES:** *blank journal books*

At the close of a meeting, give each teenager a blank journal book. Encourage kids to use the journals to record major life events and discoveries through the years. Tell kids they can make the journals heirlooms for their children and grandchildren.

Close with prayer, thanking God for the blessings of long life and asking him for insight into the bright side of aging.

## ▪ Ways to Show We Care ▪

**PURPOSE:** *to show appreciation to their parents*

**SCRIPTURE:** *Luke 2:41-52*

**SUPPLIES:** *Bibles, newsprint, and a marker*

Have kids form groups of three or four and read Luke 2:41-52.

Say: **At the end of the passage we just read, Jesus showed his appreciation to his parents by obeying them.** Ask:

● **What are other ways to show appreciation to your parents?**

Have kids brainstorm a list of ideas for showing appreciation to their parents. Encourage them to be creative; for example, they may mention ideas such as offering to host a seasonal party for their parents and their parents' friends just to show appreciation. List their ideas on newsprint.

Close by having kids thank God for their parents. Encourage kids to each choose one or two ideas and to start showing more appreciation to their parents this week.

## ▪ First-Aid Station ▪

**PURPOSE:** *to share messages of hope*

**SCRIPTURE:** *Hebrews 6:18-19*

**SUPPLIES:** *pens and large adhesive bandages*

Have everyone stand in a circle. Say: **Here are five thought provokers from the book *When the Hurt Won't Go Away,* by Paul W. Powell. As I read each statement, sit down if it makes you feel better and remain standing if it doesn't.**

● **"Usually God doesn't get us out—he gets us through."**

● **"It's not what happens to us; it's what happens in us that ultimately matters."**

● **"Our trials are not to punish us but to perfect us."**

● **"Life is not to be explained; it is to be lived."**

■ ■ ■ ■ ■ ■ ■ ■ ■ ■ ■ ■ ■ ■ ■ ■ ■ ■ ■ ■ ■ ■ ■ ■ ■ ■ ■ ■ ■ ■ ■ ■ ■ ■

● "God doesn't give us answers. He gives us himself as the answer, and that is enough."

Have all the kids sit down. Give each person a pen and two large adhesive bandages. Have each group member look at the person on his or her right and write a message of hope for that person on one of the bandages. Have each person place the bandage on the recipient's hand or cheek.

Close by having each teenager say a prayer for his or her partner then place another bandage over the first one to form a cross.

# ■ Loving God ■

**PURPOSE:** *to creatively express their love for God and others*

**SCRIPTURE:** *Deuteronomy 6:5 and Matthew 22:39*

**SUPPLIES:** *as needed*

Have kids form groups of four. Give each group freedom to use any available supplies to create an expression of love for God. For example, a group might perform a skit, write a prayer, or form a human statue representing the group's love. Have groups express their love for God in these creative ways.

Say: **The Bible calls us to love God and to love each other. Let's ask God to help us know how to love better and to act on that love in our relationships with others.**

Close with a time of silent prayer.

# ■ Put on Christ ■

**PURPOSE:** *to remember that they will live forever through Christ*

**SCRIPTURE:** *John 11:25-26; John 14:1-4; Philippians 1:21; and Hebrews 9:27-28*

**SUPPLIES:** *Bibles, heavy paper for masks, scissors, and markers*

Have each group design a mask that reflects the group's reaction to one of the following Scriptures: John 11:25-26; Philippians 1:21; and Hebrews 9:27-28. Ask:

● **What makes you happy when you think about the afterlife?**
● **What things frighten you?**

Have a volunteer read aloud John 14:1-4, then say: **While we don't know everything about what happens after we die, we do** know this: Jesus has been there and is preparing a place for us. That can give us peace.

## • Getting to Know Him •

**PURPOSE:** *to brainstorm ways to get to know Jesus better*

**SCRIPTURE:** *Philippians 3:8*

**SUPPLIES:** *paper and pencils*

Form groups of three. Give each group a sheet of paper and a pencil. Ask each group to list five things people can do to get to know Jesus better. Have each person choose one idea and share how he or she plans to carry it out in the coming weeks.

## • My Salvation •

**PURPOSE:** *to commit to telling others about the good news of eternal life*

**SCRIPTURE:** *Matthew 28:19-20*

**SUPPLIES:** *a Bible, tape, construction paper, and markers*

Read aloud Matthew 28:19-20 to your group. Give each person a sheet of construction paper and a marker. Have kids tear their paper into silhouettes of themselves. On one side of their papers, have kids write notes to God—thanking him for the gift of eternal life in heaven. On the other side, have kids write commitments to tell others the good news as commanded in Matthew 28:19-20.

Have kids tape their silhouettes to the wall. Ask them to pray silently. Then close by saying: **We don't fully understand God. Yet all the questions we can't answer today will one day be answered. Until then, let's tell others about the good news of Jesus' sacrifice for us.**

## • Resisting Is... •

**PURPOSE:** *to create a T-shirt slogan about resisting temptation*

**SCRIPTURE:** *James 1:12-15*

**SUPPLIES:** *a Bible, large black or brown plastic garbage bags, scissors, markers, white paper, and tape*

Have teenagers create T-shirts from large plastic garbage bags by cutting holes for their heads and arms.

Have kids form pairs and have partners tell each other one or two ways they resist evil (or the temptation to choose evil over good). Then have kids share their ideas with the rest of the group. Ask partners to help each other develop T-shirt slogans describing ways to resist evil. Have them write the slogans on white paper and tape them to the shirts. Then have kids put on their plastic T-shirts. Read James 1:12-15 and close in prayer, asking God to help kids resist evil and the temptation to choose evil over good.

# ▪ Yes, I'm Sent! ▪

**PURPOSE:** *to commit to ministering in the world*

**SCRIPTURE:** *Matthew 28:19 and 1 Timothy 4:12-16*

**SUPPLIES:** *"Here Am I, Send Me" handouts (p. 105) and pencils*

Distribute photocopies of the "Here Am I, Send Me" handout (p. 105) and pencils. Have kids complete the first two sections.

When kids are finished with the first two sections, say: **You probably have found several ways you can reach out to other people. As Christians, we are sent out to minister to the world. After a moment of silent prayer, read the statement at the bottom of your handout. If you can make that commitment, sign it.**

Allow students a few moments to pray silently and to sign their commitments. You may wish to give kids the option of writing "not now" on their handouts. That will take the pressure off kids to sign the commitment when they really don't mean it. No one will know who signed the commitment and who wrote, "not now."

Say: **Everyone struggles to some degree with God's desire to "send" us out into the world. But by working together and depending on God's power, we can all be the people he wants us to be.**

# ▪ A Rainstorm of a Brainstorm ▪

**PURPOSE:** *to explore ways to care for God's creation*

**SCRIPTURE:** *Psalm 104:24-25, 31*

**SUPPLIES:** *a Bible, paper, and pencils*

*(continued on p. 106)*

# Here Am I, Send Me

**Draw a box around the gifts and abilities you can use to carry out the ministry of Christ.**

| | | | |
|---|---|---|---|
| I can talk with people easily. | I can teach others about Jesus. | I am a good listener. | I usually know when someone is hurting. |
| I can pray for people. | I can build deep friendships. | I keep loving people, even when they hurt me. | I can make people feel welcome and included. |
| I can be encouraging to others. | I care about people. | I have a positive, upbeat attitude. | I have these special talents that I can use for ministry: |

**Draw a circle around ways you think God may want to use you.**

| | | | |
|---|---|---|---|
| I could share Christ's love with a non-Christian friend. | I could invite new people to our youth group. | I could befriend someone who is lonely. | I could be involved in ministry to my school campus. |
| I could be a leader in the youth group. | I could pray for hurting people. | I could encourage other Christians in their faith. | I could carry out another specific ministry: |

Lord, I want to use the gifts and abilities you have given me for your ministry. I commit to being involved in your ministry. Help me to do the things you want me to do.

Signed: _____

Form four groups. Give each group a sheet of paper and a pencil. Have each group create an "environment" acrostic, with each letter representing a way to take care of God's creation.

Have each group choose someone to read its ideas. Have each teenager mention one thing he or she can do in the coming week to take care of the environment. Read Psalm 104:24-25, 31 as a closing prayer.

You might ask for volunteers to get together during the week to combine the lists and create a handout. Ask the pastor for permission to include it as a bulletin insert, or have youth group members distribute the handouts after church services.

## • Untruth's Consequences •

**PURPOSE:** *to write covenants with God about honesty*

**SCRIPTURE:** *Psalm 15:1-3*

**SUPPLIES:** *paper, pencils, a shoe box, and tape*

Say: **Honesty isn't always easy. Sometimes lying to a friend or a parent seems like an easy way out of a situation. But lies often come back to hurt people.**

Give each teenager a sheet of paper and a pencil. Have each person write a covenant with God to work on being honest. Then have kids fold their papers and place them in a shoe box. Seal the box with tape and promise the group that the box will stay sealed. Place it in a prominent place in your meeting room to remind kids to be honest.

Have kids form pairs. Have partners take turns praying for each other. Encourage kids to work on being honest with each other and their families in the coming weeks.

## • Fix 'Em Today •

**PURPOSE:** *to try to mend broken relationships*

**SCRIPTURE:** *Matthew 4:17*

**SUPPLIES:** *paper, envelopes, stamps, and pencils*

Give each person a sheet of paper, an envelope, a stamp, and a pencil. Say: **Think about a broken relationship, such as one with a friend, a boyfriend, a girlfriend, or God. Then write a letter to that person, expressing your sincere desire to make up.**

After kids have written their letters, have them address the letters to themselves and stamp them. Say: **One way to heal a broken relationship is to talk with the person you've hurt or who has hurt you. In a week, I'll mail these letters back to you. Before that time, see what you can do to make up with the person. If you wrote your letter to God, spend the week in prayer, asking God to help you discover a new depth in your relationship.**

Collect the letters. Close in prayer, asking for God's help in healing broken relationships.

Mail the letters in one week!

## • Giving Forgiveness •

**PURPOSE:** *to replace their grudges with forgiveness*

**SCRIPTURE:** *Luke 23:33-34*

**SUPPLIES:** *Bibles*

Have kids form trios and have everyone line up against a wall. Have one person in each trio kneel on his or her hands and knees. Have the other two people (call them "grudges") sit on the kneeling person's back. Have this person try to carry both grudges at the same time to the opposite wall—without dropping either of them.

Afterward, have everyone sit down. Ask the grudge carriers:

● **How did it feel to carry your grudges?**

● **How did you feel when you finally let go of your grudges?**

Then say: **When we carry a grudge, we are weighed down. God wants us to let go of our grudges and replace them with forgiveness.**

Have kids think of people who have wronged them or people they hold grudges against. Read aloud Luke 23:33-34. Close in prayer, asking God to help each teenager forgive and love the person who has caused him or her pain.

## • Watch Your Mouth •

**PURPOSE:** *to keep commitments*

**SCRIPTURES:** *Psalm 15*

**SUPPLIES:** *a Bible, index cards, and pencils*

Say: **A commitment can be as simple as promising your mom that you'll take the trash out or as big as getting married. When** we make commitments, people depend on us, and people are hurt if we break our commitments.

Read aloud Psalm 15, emphasizing verse 4. Have each teenager write on an index card, "Keep commitments even when it hurts." Have kids put their cards at home, in places where they'll see them often.

Encourage kids to think seriously before making commitments and to keep them once they're made.

Close in prayer, asking God to give kids wisdom when they are making commitments and strength to follow through on their commitments.

# ■ True Friends ■

**PURPOSE:** *to think of people who need encouragement in their relationships with God*

**SCRIPTURE:** *Acts 4:32-37; 9:23-27; and 11:22-30*

**SUPPLIES:** *a Bible*

Read aloud Acts 4:32-37; 9:23-27; and 11:22-30. After each passage, ask how it describes encouragement. Then ask:

● **What does it mean when someone says, "A friend is someone who encourages you"?**

● **How do your friends encourage you?**

● **How do you encourage them?**

● **What does encouragement do for people?**

● **What is one thing you will do this week to encourage a friend or a family member?**

Say: **Even though he never really gets any credit for being a great leader in the Christian church, Barnabas stood by Paul when Paul needed him. Perhaps Paul couldn't have been as effective if it hadn't been for Barnabas' encouraging him from the background. When Barnabas encouraged people, they grew closer to the Lord. Think of someone who needs your encouragement to grow in his or her relationship with God.**

Close with a prayer, asking God to help each teenager encourage the person he or she thought of.

■ ■ ■ ■ ■ ■ ■ ■ ■ ■ ■ ■ ■ ■ ■ ■ ■ ■ ■ ■ ■ ■ ■ ■ ■ ■ ■ ■ ■ ■ ■ ■ ■ ■ ■ ■ ■ ■

# ▪ Hug for Hurts ▪

**PURPOSE:** *to seek comfort through Christ's promise of eternal life when loved ones die*

**SCRIPTURE:** *John 11:23-27*

**SUPPLIES:** *a Bible, index cards, and pencils*

Give each person an index card and a pencil. Say: **Write a set of initials on the card, representing a friend or a relative who has died in your lifetime.**

Take the cards and gather everyone in a group hug. As kids listen, read aloud John 11:23-27. Stop after each verse to read initials from the index cards until all the initials have been read. Close with a prayer for God's comfort when someone we love dies.

# ▪ Survey Says ▪

**PURPOSE:** *to try to predict the top five class hopes*

**SCRIPTURE:** *Hebrews 6:19*

**SUPPLIES:** *paper, pencils, and a chalkboard and chalk (or newsprint and a marker)*

Distribute sheets of paper and pencils. Ask each person to write a list of the five things they hope for most in life. Then have them write what they think are the five most hoped-for things of the people in the class. Don't let them reveal their answers to the rest of the class until everyone is finished.

Have each teenager read aloud his or her individual list, and write kids' responses on a chalkboard or on newsprint. After everyone has read his or her list, tally the results. Announce the top five class hopes and see who made the best prediction.

Write the class hopes on a chalkboard, then close with prayer, asking God to help the class strive for each hope listed.

# ▪ Jesus, Our Example ▪

**PURPOSE:** *to follow Jesus' example of unselfishness*

**SCRIPTURE:** *Philippians 2:5-8*

**SUPPLIES:** *pencils, index cards, tape, newsprint, and a marker*

Give each person a pencil and an index card. Say: **On your card, write one area in which you have a tendency to be selfish—an area you want God to help you with; for example, taking for granted your home and all the food you need to survive.**

While kids are writing, tape a sheet of newsprint to a wall and draw a large cross on it. Ask a volunteer to read aloud Philippians 2:5-8. Ask:

● **What does this passage say about Jesus' unselfish example?**

Say: **Jesus was God, yet he humbled himself to the point of giving up his own life for us. That's an example of unselfish living that will never be topped.**

Say: **Let's give up the areas of selfishness you've written on your cards. One at a time, tape your card to this cross.**

Pause while kids do this. Then have kids close their eyes while you pray: **God, help us uproot all selfishness in our lives and live as Jesus did—unselfishly giving to others. Amen.**

# ▪ Awesome God ▪

**PURPOSE:** *to brainstorm ways to live as God wants them to*

**SCRIPTURE:** *2 Thessalonians 1:6-11*

**SUPPLIES:** *Bibles, markers, and newsprint*

Have groups read 2 Thessalonians 1:6-11 then think of ways to live life as God wants us to; for example, "Tell others about Jesus" or "Reach out to needy, lonely people." Have them write the ideas on newsprint.

Give each person a marker. Say: **God wants us to live life for him. Reread these newsprint lists. Circle one way you want to live life for God this next week. Then sign your initials near the idea.**

Have kids form a large circle and join hands for a closing prayer. When you pause during the prayer, have kids offer to God the ways they'll live life for him. Pray: **God, help us be strong and live our lives as you want us to. Hear us as we tell the ways we will do this.** Pause. **Thank you for Jesus and for giving us the gift of eternal life in heaven. Amen.**

# Scripture Index